THE FIFTY DAYS

THE FIFTY DAYS

Napoleon in England

JEAN DUHAMEL

Translated by R. A. Hall

UNIVERSITY OF MIAMI PRESS
Coral Gables Florida

to my friend

JAMES DILL SMITH

PUBLISHERS' NOTE

The English translation of this book had been almost completed
by the late Mr R. A. Hall before his death, with the exception of a
few passages and the texts of a number of letters and documents
which had appeared in a French version in M. Duhamel's original
book, first published in 1963. The English texts from which M.
Duhamel had worked were unfortunately destroyed after publica-
tion, so that considerable further research was necessary in order
to re-establish their correct form and *provenance*. Some of this
work was carried out under Mr Hall's direction before his death;
the many remaining gaps in the documents and in the translation
have been most capably filled by Mrs Jocelyn Pagan.

CONTENTS

LIST OF ILLUSTRATIONS

(between pages 64 and 65)

Foreword

IT IS APPROPRIATE that English readers should have this book, which fills a definite gap in our knowledge of Napoleon's exile after Waterloo, and describes how Napoleon missed his only chance of setting foot on English soil. It is written with the clarity and brilliance to be expected from a distinguished French historian, who is also familiar with English legal procedure.

The story told by Monsieur Jean Duhamel brings out the peculiar and unique embarrassment of the situation created by Napoleon's surrender to Captain Maitland of the *Bellerophon* and his famous 'Themistocles' letter to the Prince Regent. Napoleon had been a crowned and anointed sovereign, yet he had been declared an outlaw and 'enemy of the human race' by the Congress of Vienna. In the circumstances Lord Eldon's advice to the Government that his status was that of a prisoner of war was reasonable and judicious. At least it averted the dire possibility of handing Napoleon over to the Bourbons to be shot like Ney.

Napoleon was capable of great self-deception in his later years, but even he could hardly have seriously believed that he would be allowed to live as a country gentleman in England, as his brother Lucien had been allowed to do between 1809 and 1814. The British Government's relations with the European powers, and particularly the Bourbon government they were trying to establish in France, would have been ruined. Napoleon's letter to the Prince Regent was probably a bluff, a gamble, a forlorn hope, for as he remarked to Marchand when he signed the letter 'There is always a danger in entrusting oneself to one's enemies but it is better to risk relying on their sense of honour than to be in their hands as a prisoner of war'.

Napoleon in England would inevitably have been a source of political intrigue. Monsieur Duhamel's account of the activities of Capell Lofft, one of the Foxite Whigs, is an example from one angle. The attitude of the man in the street, whether military or civilian, is shown by the feelings of the crew of the *Bellerophon* and

of the crowds at Plymouth. Despite the never-ending wars to stop
Napoleon's bid for world conquest, despite the crude war propaganda of the Tory press, they sensed that they were in the presence
of a unique historical personality, and they were not unaware that
Napoleon stood for the repudiation of oligarchy and the career
open to talents. As Wellington later remarked, 'Napoleon was not a
personality but a principle'. And Lord Palmerston reminded
Queen Victoria that 'Napoleon Buonaparte, the greatest enemy
that England ever had, was treated with respect while at Plymouth
and with consideration while at St Helena.'

Napoleon's exile at St Helena lies beyond the scope of this book,
but Palmerston's judgment may be accepted, with the proviso that
it was not ill-will but sheer stupidity on the part of Lord Bathurst
which led to the appointment of Sir Hudson Lowe as Governor of
St Helena. His sole distinction had been to command the Corsican
Rangers, a battalion of royalist emigrés and the appointment of a
man with his background was an insult Napoleon could neither
understand nor forgive.

Felix Markham
Hertford College, Oxford

Introduction

*The times are past when History could
be tailored to suit some thesis
or honest prejudice.*

OCTAVE AUBRY

THOUGH works on Napoleon are legion, some episodes in his life
are obscure. Thus something still needs to be said about the brief
period that began the evening after Waterloo on 18 June, 1815, and
ended on the following 9 August in Plymouth Sound, when the
fallen monarch began his voyage to St Helena.

Have historians, in studying these fifty days, succeeded in
establishing all the considerations that weighed with Napoleon
when he gave himself up on board the English cruiser off the Île
d'Aix? Have they paid sufficient attention to the spirit of his
famous letter of 13 July, 1815, sent to the Prince Regent before
repairing on board H.M.S. *Bellerophon,* in which he writes of his
'most powerful, most persevering and most generous foe?' Have
they weighed the words of his appeal to the magnanimity of
England and to the laws of that country which safeguard individual
liberty? What did he know about *Habeas Corpus*? Did he expect
anything to come of it? Had he read Voltaire, who in his 'Letters'
had been the first to explain to his fellow-countrymen this
characteristically insular embodiment of legislation and legal
theory, which he described as the bulwark of liberty? Did Napoleon
expect asylum under the protection of these laws? Would they
operate in his favour? And, events having belied his expectations, had
he been advised of the obstacles set up by English law which he was
later to encounter? Satisfactory answers do not seem to have been
given to these embarrassing questions which have never been the
subject of systematic enquiry. Indeed, they have often been avoided
by writers unwilling to lose themselves in the maze of English law.

Neither, on the other hand, have the circumstances immediately
surrounding the surrender of Napoleon to the English been
completely cleared up. There are two opposing views: some think

that Napoleon was deceived and trapped by the captain of *Bellerophon* – a view that Napoleon was himself at pains to express. Others, on the contrary, are inclined to believe in the good faith of Captain Maitland, and are of the opinion that the Emperor, hunted by Louis XVIII's police, had no illusions when he embarked. Other authors vacillate, and by trying to combine the two theories, arrive at no conclusion. These interesting questions, however distorted by national sentiments, will not be lost on the reader who eschews myth and prefers established fact. Since these complex problems became intermingled during the period under review, it is necessary to disentangle and analyse them, by dividing them up, in the accepted way, into as many parts as possible. By these means we hope to arrive at a clear and faithful account of a little-known and obscure part of the Napoleonic epic. The English archives have been useful, because although they have already been studied by historians of the Empire, the latter have found it difficult to make full use of them on particular points, without running the risk of distorting the proportions of their own works. In our case, on the other hand, since our work only begins at Waterloo and ends before St Helena, we have been able to bring to light important documents and to give due weight to facts hitherto regarded as secondary. It is as if – drawing an analogy from the cinema – we had taken from a film covering the entire life of Napoleon a long passage which brought out sharply events after the last hours of Waterloo and Paris – the arrival at Rochefort; the Île d'Aix; the masts of *Bellerophon* flying the White Ensign and multi-coloured signal flags; the inaccessible coast of England; the hazards of *Habeas Corpus* proceedings. In this way it is possible to feel one is at the centre of events, to observe at close quarters the actors in a great drama, the look in their eyes, 'warts and all'. A fascinating task when one remembers it deals with the most tragic moments of the Emperor's life, when his ultimate destiny was decided. The importance of this phase is in inverse proportion to its length.

Such will be the approach of this work. If it fills in some gaps, if it casts some light on certain aspects of the Emperor's last days in Europe before his sad departure, and if it helps us to understand them better, the author feels he will have performed a service in the cause of historical truth.

Jean Duhamel

THE FIFTY DAYS

CHAPTER I

Downfall

*A cloud, crossing the sky in the wrong direction, was
sufficient to bring about the collapse of a world.*

VICTOR HUGO

ON 1 MARCH, 1815, Napoleon after escaping from Elba landed
near Antibes. Hastening by rapid stages to Paris, he entered the
Tuileries through one door as Louis XVIII was leaving through
the other.

The man whose arena had been Europe had felt stifled in his
Lilliputian kingdom. The victors had snatched from him his wife
and son. A rumour had reached him that the Allies, disturbed by
his dangerous proximity, were contemplating banishing him to
the Azores, perhaps to St Helena, a name which was now beginning to be canvassed. The Emperor was even apprehensive that he
might be assassinated. Had not Brulart, one of Cadoudal's officers,
been appointed Governor of Corsica? His presence was suspect,
more especially as Napoleon was finding himself compelled to
discharge *grognards* of his Old Guard, his one protection against
any attack, through lack of funds to pay them. Indeed the French
Treasury did not pay him the allowances provided for by the
Treaty of Fontainebleau. Furthermore, was it not tempting to
strike a telling blow in the face of the many mistakes of the
Restoration Government? In short, ambition is a thirst that is
never quenched, like the desire for revenge.

Immediately on his return the Emperor was lavish with reassuring statements and declarations of peaceful intentions, but in
vain. The Allies united. From that moment he was treated like a
criminal who had broken his bail and would on recapture be
killed the moment his identity was established. He had torn up
the Treaty of Fontainebleau of 11 April, 1814, and with it his only
title to his life. He became an outlaw in Europe. Such was the
implacable and unanimous declaration of 15 March, 1815,
implemented by the Treaty of Vienna in the same month.

The boldness of the escape from Elba resulted in a renewal of the Coalition. That was the situation the Emperor had to face. He had behind him the support of a country which, for the most part, was disillusioned with the Bourbons, and which, after the humiliation of the previous year, wished to avenge its defeat. In a few weeks Napoleon raised a powerful army of 125,000 men. He had recovered the power of decision which had deserted him during the Russian campaign and conceived a plan which was as bold as it was sound. As with his early campaigns, it provided for the separate defeat in detail of the Anglo–Dutch and Prussian armies, his present enemies, already concentrated and menacing in Flanders; afterwards turning on Schwarzenberg, the head of whose columns lay already on the Rhine. The Russians, further away still, would be dealt with later. Eluding Wellington and Blücher, Napoleon reached the road to Charleroi, and was thus in a position, when opportunity offered, to deal with either separately. He turned to face Blücher and beat him at Ligny, but first Ney's indecision at Quatre-Bras and then Drouet d'Erlon's failure to come up in time deprived him of the considerable fruits he might have expected from this victory. Obliged to detach Grouchy and some 30,000 men in pursuit of Blücher, this did not prevent him marching at once against Wellington. He was well on the way to success at Mount St Jean, but the attack began late owing to rain; while Grouchy maintained that he had received no clear orders, and remained deaf, despite the urging of Gérard, to the noise of gunfire. The Emperor was thus exposed on the flank to a resolute attack by Blücher, who refused to consider himself beaten, and marched his troops to bring help to Wellington.

The great planner of battles who had some weeks earlier lost Berthier, his best Chief of Staff ('if I had had Berthier with me, I would not have suffered this reverse'), and had declined Murat's offers of service when his assistance might have been decisive — Murat would not have hazarded his cavalry like Ney — now thought he could finish off Wellington with a decisive stroke, and threw in every last man of his reserves, instead of breaking off the engagement. The results were disastrous.

The evening of that terrible day, escorted by the remnants of the Old Guard and accompanied by a slender retinue, the Emperor returned to Paris in a post chaise; his own coach had been captured.

Once in Paris, Napoleon was advised by Davout to prorogue both

Chambers of the Assembly, which in Carnot's view would vote
him plenary powers. Fouché knew they would not agree to this
course but feigned agreement with Carnot. At the same time, with
characteristic duplicity, he persuaded Regnault, a supporter of the
Emperor, to suggest to Napoleon that he abdicate in favour of his
son and to enlist the support of Marshal Davout and Lucien
Bonaparte for this course. Then, acting as he usually did
through an intermediary, he prompted La Fayette to propose to
both Chambers that they sit permanently. They hesitated for
some time but in the end decided on Napoleon's abdication pure
and simple; and at the same time appointed a Commission of
Government, presided over by Fouché, consisting of five members, three deputies and two peers. At this juncture Napoleon
could have brought off a successful *coup d'etat* with the aid
of his many partisans, who acclaimed him even after his defeat
and in Paris still demonstrated in his favour. However, he nobly
declined to try. Then Fouché, seizing his opportunity, sent Davout
to him with the invitation to take refuge in Malmaison. The
Emperor received the Marshal extremely coldly but agreed in the
end to accept surveillance by General Count Becker.[1]

By such manœuvres Fouché eliminated Napoleon, whose
energy and general state of health had been sopped by the strains
of the recent campaign. Napoleon had also hoped, by sacrificing
himself, to preserve the crown for his son. Fouché basely entertained the idea of handing him over to the Allies; then he resolved
to suggest to the Emperor, knowing that he too had the same idea,
that he leave for the United States. A division of two frigates would
await him at Rochefort; at the same time safe-conducts would be
sought from the English. However, he enjoined the captains of
these units to sail only if the safe-conducts reached them, which
was unlikely. Finally, he instructed General Becker to press on
energetically with the arrangements for the Emperor's departure.

In the avenues of Malmaison, attended by Madame Mère and
Queen Hortense—and the shade of Joséphine—his hand thrust
into his waistcoat, against a place which was already painful,

[1] Léonard Nicholas Becker, or Bajert-Becker, Count of Mons (1770–1840)
served in the San Domingo and Italian campaigns. Commanded a division
at Austerlitz. Elected to the Chamber of Deputies, 1815. Peer of France,
1819.

Napoleon strolled up and down, surrounded by his faithful companions in adversity, Las Cases, Marshal Bertrand, Savary, General Lallemand,[1] Montholon, Planat de la Faye.[2] Trapped as they were, they indulged in endless arguments. Some saw safety in the United States, a hospitable country which had been at war from 1812 to 1814 because she refused to submit to the Orders in Council which (in reply to the Continental System) had prohibited trade with France. Others, including Las Cases, leaned towards England. La Valette and Caulaincourt, if consulted, would both have agreed with Las Cases and would have added that every foreigner landing in England thereby became entitled to the protection of her liberal laws. But what justification had La Valette and Caulaincourt for speaking with such assurance? And how could they decide, when it was problematical whether even safe-conducts would be forthcoming? Anyway, was it certain what attitude the British would take?

Actually, Napoleon should have been already on his way to the Atlantic coast, but he still could not make up his mind. Before leaving for Rochefort he hesitated what course to take. There was another reason for his delay. Napoleon had no intention of leaving without baggage or without supplies. He wished to take his effects with him—his books, gold and silver plate, souvenirs, specie. He needed time to load his wagons. Since 21 June he had taken steps to build up a store of valuables.

One morning the Emperor heard Blücher's guns, now at

[1] Baron Charles François Antoine Lallemand, (1774–1839) one of two brother generals of the same name. Enlisted as a volunteer in 1792, took part in all the French campaigns during the Revolution and Empire. Appointed military governor of Laon and of the Department of the Aisne by Louis XVIII, he rallied to the Emperor when he returned from Elba. Commanded the artillery of the Guard at Waterloo. Followed Napoleon to Malmaison and Rochefort. The English refused him permission to accompany Napoleon to St Helena and imprisoned him for a time. He then went to the United States, whence, after a time, he returned to France.

[2] Nicholas Louis Planat de la Faye (1784–1864). Scion of a Royalist family, entered the Army through necessity in 1803 and took part in the principal campaigns under the Empire. Aide-de-camp to Lariboisière (who died at Königsberg during the Russian campaign). Then attached to Drouot who lent him to the Emperor from time to time in 1813 to 1814 to act as his A.D.C. During the Hundred Days Planat remained faithful to Napoleon and embarked in *Bellerophon*. He tried in vain to accompany the Emperor to St Helena. Imprisoned with Savary at Malta. Back on the Continent he became A.D.C. to Prince Eugène. When Marmont attacked the latter in his Memoirs Planat successfully vindicated him.

Chatou. With his unerring eye for an opening he saw he could surprise the Marshal, now separated from Wellington, in the very act of manœuvring. His spirit was roused; he wanted to defeat his old enemy. He offered his service as a simple general 'in good faith as a soldier, a citizen and a Frenchman'. This proposal only succeeded in exasperating Fouché, who sent him, through Becker, a formal order to leave. Napoleon put on civilian dress, donned a round hat, and took an affectionate farewell of Queen Hortense. He gave her his wedding ring; and in parting she besought him to accept as a last gift her diamond necklace. Then he set off in his barouche and spent that night at Rambouillet. It was 29 June. From Rambouillet he went via Vendôme, Tours, Poitiers, St Maixent, arriving at Niort on 1 July. On 3 July, the day Paris capitulated, he was at Rochefort. He wished to spare France further horrors.

The choice of Rochefort as the port of embarkation was, to say the least, surprising. Why, since Admiral Decrès had advised departure through Le Havre, did Fouché select this port for the fallen monarch? It was the one port in France which the English force, with relatively weak armament, could most easily blockade. As everyone knows, it is covered by three islands, Oléron, Ré and Aix. To sail out of Rochefort, a ship must use one of the channels separating these islands from the mainland, either the Antioch, the Maumusson or, with La Rochelle abeam, the Breton narrows. Some bay on the Atlantic coast in which the frigates could moor discreetly, and from which they could easily put to sea, seemed indicated. But Fouché, with Machiavellian calculation, probably had it in mind to cast the Emperor into the jaws of the English wolf, perhaps the least bloody of the Allies. He undoubtedly desired the elimination, not the death, of the Emperor.

The first action of Napoleon on arrival at Rochefort was to ✳ enquire about the frigates. They were indeed there; the *Saale*,[1] commanded by Captain Philibert[2] the senior officer, and the

---

[1] 40 guns, completed in 1810.

[2] Pierre Henri Philibert (1774–1824). Entered the service in 1786. Commanded one of the lighters at Boulogne. Served in Martinique, Domingo, the Indies and in Asian waters. Promoted captain in 1820.

Méduse,[1] whose name was to acquire a sad notoriety, commanded by Captain Ponée.[2] But Philibert, to the great disappointment of the Emperor, had not received the proposed safe-conducts and his instructions were to wait for them. Furthermore, the wind was adverse. Ponée, a gallant officer, was prepared to sail with the next wind, but he was under Philibert's command.

Admiral Martin,[3] an old sea dog, living in retirement at Rochefort and devoted to the Emperor, was called in for consultation, and put forward a plan which had the merit of originality. This was to make Tremblade in a long-boat, then press on to Royan at full speed, and there embark in the frigate *Bayadère*,[4] which was lying at anchor in the Gironde under a resolute captain, Baudin,[5] who would undertake to convey the Emperor to America.

In the same area Napoleon would find, besides the *Bayadère*, the *Pike* and *Ludlow*, fast American merchantmen, about to sail for New York. But Napoleon would have to make up his mind, which he was reluctant to do.

This lack of resolution contrasts with the drive shown by the British, evidenced by the arrival of a major naval unit, *Bellerophon*,[6] 74 guns, commanded by Captain Frederick

---

[1] A 44-gun frigate, built in 1810, she was ordered, in 1816 together with the corvette *L'Écho*, the brig *Argus* and the long-ship *Loire* to transport to Sénégal (which England had restored to France under the 1814 and 1815 treaties) the new government, its officials, and troops. This little squadron sailed on 17 June, 1816. Having parted company from the other ships, the *Méduse*, thanks to the incompetence of her captain, de Roy de Chaumarez, foundered on the Arguin Bank on 2 June, 1816. This terrible wreck was the subject of the well-known painting by Géricault.

[2] François Ponée (1775–1863). Entered the service in 1794; took part in numerous campaigns under the Directory, Consulate and Empire, at San Domingo in the Indies and off the French coast. Retired with the rank of captain in 1831.

[3] Count Pierre Martin (1752–1820). Entered the service in 1769, took part in the Île de France and Savannah campaigns. Promoted rear-admiral in 1793, he was given command of the Mediterranean Fleet and landed in Corsica. Fought an action against Admiral Hotham (uncle of the admiral of the same name mentioned in this work) off Hyères. Created Count in 1810.

[4] 24-gun frigate, built in 1810.

[5] Charles Baudin, son of a member of the Convention. Devoted to the Empire, he left the Navy in 1815 to start up in business at Le Havre. Rejoining the service in 1830, he attained the highest rank, Admiral of France, a few days before his death.

[6] The *Bellerophon* was a vessel of 1,613 tons with 74 guns, built in 1786. Present at Aboukir, where she sustained severe damage in action with the *Orient*. Also present at Trafalgar.

Maitland,[1] followed by some smaller ships, *Daphne*, *Slaney* and
Myrmidon.[2] These watch-dogs arrived in the nick of time to stand
between the Emperor and the open sea.

The timely presence of a well-armed English naval force must be
attributed to the fact that the Admiralty knew its business. If
Napoleon's strategy on land was brilliant, at sea that of the
Admiralty, though less spectacular, was superior. How can twenty
years of unbroken success be explained otherwise? Trafalgar had
defeated the whole purpose of the camp at Boulogne. His Majesty's
ships were everywhere, whenever and wherever they were needed,
in India, the Antilles, off the Spanish coast and in the Straits of
Dover; a remarkable state of affairs when one remembers the
slowness and difficulty of communication in those days. An order
was less likely to be drawn up carelessly when a ship, once it had
sailed, could rarely be recalled to receive a counter-order.

Hence, as soon as Waterloo was won, the Admiralty without
delay disposed the fleet as the circumstances of the hour demanded.
Sailors with years of service, clear-sighted, bending over their
maps in Whitehall or gathered around their enormous mahogany
tables sending instructions to impetuous admirals stationed all
over the globe, already regarded Napoleon as finished. As he could
not stay in France without risking arrest and execution by the
Allies, he was obviously going to try to escape. And how? By sea,
of course. The Admiralty stationed forces from Le Havre to the
Gulf of Gascony under Admiral Lord Keith,[3] commanding in

---

[1] Sir Frederick Lewis Maitland (1777–1839). Born at Rankeilour, Fife. The
bravery he displayed while serving under Lord Howe in 1794 gained him
promotion as commander of a sloop. Taken prisoner by the Spaniards in 1799,
he took part next in the Egyptian campaign. During the war he proved to be an
excellent officer and he had several important captures to his credit. In 1814 he
was given command of *Bellerophon*. Knighted after the surrender of Napoleon.
Rear-Admiral in 1830. Appointed Commander-in-Chief East Indies Squadron
in 1837. Died on board his flagship *Wellesley* off Bombay.

[2] *Slaney* and *Myrmidon* were small sixth-rate ships, or corvettes, recently
built, of 20 guns. *Daphne* was of the same class, but somewhat older.

[3] George Elphinstone, Viscount Keith (1746–1823) belonged to the old
Scottish family of Elphinstone. A distinguished seaman who first saw action in
the American War of Independence. Captured the Malgue fort during the siege
of Toulon in 1793. Raised the Union Jack at the Cape of Good Hope and in
Ceylon. Negotiated with Menou the evacuation of the French from Egypt and
fought them at sea all through the Napoleonic period. His daughter later married
Comte Flahaut de la Billarderie, aide-de-camp to the Emperor and a political

that area, with the task of watching the French coast. These initial precautions were completely justified. From the end of June reports started to reach London that Napoleon, frustrated at Malmaison, intended to leave for Rochefort. Acting on that intelligence, the Admiralty had only to tighten its net by concentrating a squadron between La Rochelle and the estuary of the Gironde. Rear Admiral Sir Henry Hotham[1] was appointed to command because of his familiarity with the Atlantic coast. Having hoisted his flag in *Superb*[2] Hotham stationed himself off Quiberon Bay and at the same time ordered Maitland, who also knew these waters, to lie off Rochefort to watch the two frigates that had been promised to the Emperor. It was a most disturbing disposition for anyone trying to leave France.

The *Bellerophon* was certainly an old ship but 'Billy Ruffian' (as her ship's company dubbed her), was a formidable fighting unit and capable of inflicting considerable damage on the *Saale* and the *Méduse* if their captains took it into their heads to put to sea. Her armament was manned by experienced gunners, whilst her seamen—the crew included men who had been pressed into service in the public houses of the London slums by recruiting sergeants plying them with strong drink—were a frightening lot. The officers were of aristocratic background, the men subjected to an iron discipline imposed from above by the Admiralty and transmitted through all levels of the hierarchy even down to the men in irons in the hold, and those who were flogged with the cat-o'-nine tails, often for trivial offences, their wounds afterwards being rubbed with coarse salt so that they might heal more quickly.

These were the obstacles facing Napoleon. He turned the question of escape over and over in his mind; as he could not use

refugee in London after the Hundred Days. It was this which made the fifth Marquess of Lansdowne remark one day, in the course of conversation with M. Delcassé, that he had French blood in his veins; perhaps even Talleyrand's, given that Talleyrand was Gen. Flahaut's natural father.

[1] Sir Henry Hotham (1777–1833) nephew of the distinguished sailor, Lord Hotham, on whose staff he began his career. Present at the siege of Toulon, on board *Victory*. After Trafalgar, he succeeded in capturing the few French ships which got away. Rear-Admiral 1814. A Sea Lord of the Admiralty from 1828 to 1830. Commander-in-Chief, Mediterranean Fleet, 1831. Died at Malta.

[2] *Superb* was a ship of the same class as *Bellerophon,* but more recent.

French frigates, there seemed to be no satisfactory solution. Any shabby or secret course he ruled out, not wishing to leave his brave companions behind and expose them to reprisals: such an idea was repugnant to him.

A Captain Besson, son-in-law of a Danish ship-owner, and in command of a ship (the *Magdeleine*), which had put in to load a cargo of Cognac, and was about to sail for the United States and run the English blockade, also offered his services; but the offer came to nothing. Had his ship been searched, Besson meant to hide the Emperor in a cask.

Indecision was fatal. The government in Paris, drawing strength from the present remoteness of Napoleon, felt surer of their ground and resolved from then on to act in accordance with the decision of the previous March: that is, to arrest Napoleon, notwithstanding his warm reception in Charente, where he was applauded by large crowds.

On 7 July, in the face of these threats, and still without any definite plan, Napoleon decided to leave the French mainland for the Île d'Aix where he would feel more secure. Accordingly, accompanied by his band of faithful followers, whose numbers had by now swollen to sixty-four, and his baggage, cared for by his chief valet, Marchand, he made his way to the little port of Fouras, north of Rochefort, intending to cross to the island. The heavy sea, however, compelled him to take shelter on board the *Saale*. Next day, the weather having improved, he went as far as Aix, where he would have the protection of a garrison of loyal members of the Guard. But on returning to the *Saale* he could not fail to notice the equivocal attitude of her captain, Philibert. The latter was not the sort of seaman who would make for the open sea at this juncture. Furthermore, he had orders the nature of which the Emperor could only guess. Philibert was capable of surrendering the Emperor to anyone, English or French. In the circumstances, Napoleon's best course for the time being was to leave the *Saale* and make for the fort on Aix. Meanwhile, through the glass which had scanned so many battlefields, he descried the English ships, looking like giant bumblebees at their manœuvres in the vicinity— formidable to the eye and relentlessly vigilant. As it happened, their vigilance had been intensified. Fresh and peremptory instructions had just reached Captain Maitland. The Admiralty

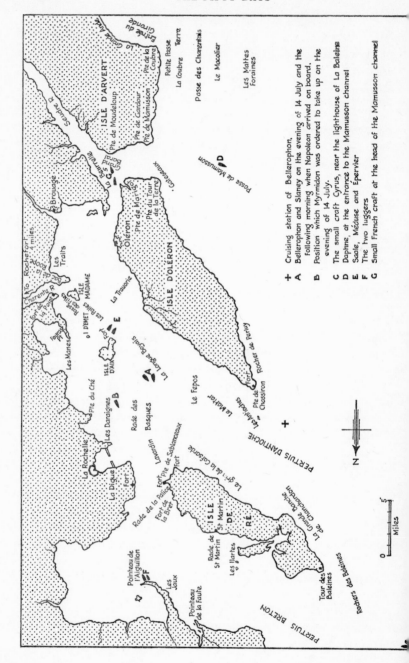

+   Cruising station of Bellerophon.
A   Bellerophon and Slaney on the evening of 14 July and the
    following morning when Napoleon arrived on board.
B   Position which Myrmidon was ordered to take up on the
    evening of 14 July.
C   The small craft Cyrus, near the lighthouse of La Baleine.
D   Daphne, at the entrance to the Mamusson channel
E   Saale, Méduse and Epervier
F   The two luggers
G   Small French craft at the head of the Mamusson channel

had received further intelligence, and lost no time in issuing this general signal:

> The Lords Commissioners of the Admiralty[1] having every reason to believe that Napoleon Bonaparte meditates his escape with his family from France to America, you are hereby required and directed, in pursuance of orders from their Lordships, signified to me by Admiral the Rt Honourable Viscount Keith, to keep the most vigilant look-out for the purpose of intercepting him, and to make the strictest search of any vessel you may fall in with.

And the order goes on:

> ... if you should be so fortunate as to intercept him, you are to transfer him and his family to the ship you command and there keep him in careful custody and return to the nearest port in England, going into Torbay in preference to Plymouth, with all possible expedition, and on your arrival you are not to permit any communication with the shore.

Napoleon therefore found himself trapped between Scylla and Charybdis. On the one hand he faced a French Government increasingly hostile as its strength grew, and on the other the Royal Navy. A formal order of arrest despatched from Paris by a special messenger, Captain de Rigny, had just reached Rochefort. And there was still no news of the safe conducts. What should they do? The Emperor, quite rightly, considered the sailing of the *Saale* and the *Méduse* out of the question: the Emperor dismissed the thought of the *Bayadère*, the *Magdeleine* and her cask: the Emperor did not wish to be the sole passenger in any ship whatever. The Emperor would leave with his household and his effects in a dignified manner. These decisions, which do him credit, ruled out all schemes which if rapidly put into effect might have been preferable. All things considered, the English card was the only one he had left to play. The *Bellerophon* came to represent the bridge that would enable the Emperor to leave France, come what may, and while it was still possible; and as a last resort to seek the hospitality of England.

Though Napoleon could hardly be favourably disposed towards

---

[1] The Lords Commissioners of the Admiralty constituted the Board of Admiralty which functioned from the reign of George III until it was absorbed in the Ministry of Defence in 1964. The Board discharged the office of Lord High Admiral.

the nation he failed to conquer, he could still appreciate her
qualities and could adapt himself to her customs. Moreover, had
not England been a haven for political refugees, such as those who
in France were in peril of a *lettre de cachet*? Had not Saint
Évremond lived for many happy years beside the Thames, the
confidant of kings? He was even buried in Westminster Abbey
Later, at the time of the Revocation of the Edict of Nantes,
the Huguenots in a body had been given permission to settle in
London. Paoli, at the time of the union of Corsica and France,
came to England and lived there peacefully. He was even given a
pension by the Government. During the French Revolution, a host
of *émigrés* had found refuge in London, and a refuge free from
molestation. Las Cases himself bore witness to this, having lived
across the Channel from 1791 to 1799. In his present predica
ment Las Cases had the ear of Napoleon, who at Fontainebleau
in 1814 had applied to Lord Castlereagh, though unsuccessfully
for permission to enter British territory.

The idea of a solution along these lines commended itself more
and more to Napoleon. One section of his party favoured it, while
another was always against it. Two factions sprang up. On the
one hand Lallemand, Montholon and Planat de la Faye opposed
the plan; so too did Gourgaud, though he later changed his mind
while Bertrand (yielding to the nagging of his Irish wife),
Savary and Las Cases were in favour of it. Faced with these
conflicting views, the only thing to do was to sound out the
attitude of the English squadron before making a final decision.
That step was taken. Napoleon sent emissaries to the *Bellerophon*
Savary was chosen because of his experience of high office, and
Las Cases because he had some knowledge of English, which he
concealed at first (a somewhat shabby deception, this) the better
to surprise his interlocutors.

CHAPTER 2

The Emperor Surrenders

Rule, Britannia! Britannia, rule the waves!

WHILE THE EMPEROR and his companions were debating inter-
minably as to the best course to take, Captain Maitland kept watch
at the entrance to Rochefort harbour, taking advantage of the wind
or dropping anchor, as requisite. Not only were his orders from
the Admiralty crystal clear, but he also had information from the
numerous spies in the area who were in the pay of England.
Napoleon's whereabouts were known, he was a fugitive closely
pursued by minions of the Provisional Government; he wanted
to get away at all costs. And at all costs he must be prevented
from so doing, prevented from making the open sea. Topmen in
the *Bellerophon*'s crow's-nest, and look-outs in the smaller ships,
eyes glued to telescopes, scanned the coast. As the hunter waits
for his quarry at the edge of the wood, Maitland waited for the
Emperor to start the chase. Yet he was anxious, for he considered the forces at his disposal inadequate to block all three of
the channels leading out to sea.

All this time Maitland was unaware that the Emperor wished to
make contact with him. But communication with the *Bellerophon*
needed the help of some light craft — hence the co-operation of
General Becker, who was under the orders of the Provisional
Government. Becker, who was well disposed to the Emperor,
would have turned a blind eye to some secret escape plan, but in
his official capacity he could only act in accordance with his
instructions. An order had just been received from Paris enjoining
him to hasten the departure of the frigates (now no longer able to
get under way) or, should Napoleon wish to give himself up to the
British, to see him safely embarked or landed in England, the
captain of the French vessel detailed for such a task to be under
the orders of General Becker.

Such was the situation on 9 July when Count Bertrand sent the
following letter to General Becker:

Sir,

The Emperor has commanded me to request you to despatch an envoy to the British squadron, in accordance with your instructions, to inquire whether the safe-conducts requested for our voyage to the United States have now arrived.

BERTRAND
Grand Marshal

Only after he had a written order from General Becker did Captain Philibert agree to put a small ship at the Emperor's disposal.

Imagine Captain Maitland's surprise when, on the morning of 10 July, he saw from his quarter-deck a skiff making its way towards him under a flag of truce. It bore Savary and Las Cases who presented themselves as Napoleon's representatives. Savary had orders to hand the following letter addressed to Admiral Hotham, the British Commander:

9 July, 1815

Sir,

The Emperor Napoleon having abdicated the throne of France, and chosen the United States of America as a retreat, is, with his suite, at present embarked on board the two frigates which are in this port, for the purpose of proceeding to his destination. He expects a passport from the British Government, which has been promised to him, and which induces me to send the present flag of truce, to enquire of you, Sir, if you have any knowledge of the above-mentioned passport, or if you think it is the intention of the British Government to throw any impediment in the way of our voyage to the United States. I shall feel much obliged by your giving me any information you may possess on the subject.

I have directed the bearers of this letter to present to you my thanks, and to apologise for any trouble it may cause.

I have the honour to be,
Your Excellency's Most Obedient etc. etc.

BERTRAND
Grand Marshal

Actually, under the pretext of asking if the safe conduct had arrived, Napoleon, disgusted with Philibert, was anxious to sound out the attitude of the members of the British force. On this subject, however, the commander of the *Bellerophon* kept his own counsel despite the envoy's repeated enquiries. Being under Admiral Hotham's command he wanted to wait for the latter's despatches, already on the way in a fast ship, the *Falmouth*, whose spars were already visible on the horizon. Maitland played for time by asking the Frenchmen to dinner. Meantime the *Falmouth* had joined him and discharged her mails.

Admiral Hotham wrote to Maitland informing him that on 30 June the British Government had received a request from the French Government for safe-conducts to enable Bonaparte to proceed to the United States. This request was refused and Lord Keith enjoined the strictest watch to be kept by the ships under his command. In England it was thought likely that Bonaparte might escape through a Channel port. 'That is not my view', wrote Hotham, 'I have every reason to believe that he has left for Rochefort and that he will embark in one of the two frigates there.'

In the same bag Maitland found a second letter from the Admiral with the information that the French Minister of Marine had been instructed to place the two frigates at the disposal of Bonaparte and his staff. Both Houses of the French Parliament had been informed that he had left the capital on 29 June, apparently for Rochefort. Admiral Hotham considered that the two frigates were there for Bonaparte's use and it was Captain Maitland's responsibility to take all proper steps to intercept the fugitive on whose capture depended the peace of Europe.

Thus read Admiral Hotham's instructions. He was lying off Quiberon, ready for any eventuality but announcing his intention to make for Rochefort in his most powerful ship, the *Superb*. Maitland now felt able to answer the questions of the French envoys. After long discussions he wrote to his superior as follows:

Sir,

I send back the *Falmouth* without a moment's loss of time, with the accompanying dispatch which I received this morning by a schooner bearing a flag of truce, from the hands of the Duc de Rovigo and Count de Las Cases, two of Bonaparte's most attached friends. I likewise send my answer, which I have given to gain time, as I do not of course wish that Bonaparte should be aware there are such strict orders respecting him.

In the same letter Captain Maitland reported that the two envoys had tried to convince him that the peace of Europe depended on the Emperor leaving without incident and had even insinuated that, if the safe-conducts were not forthcoming, the frigates would

attempt to escape. To which Captain Maitland replied that he
would resist such a step with all available force. He believed that
Napoleon wished to go to a neutral country in the frigates, but if
the frigates came out he would direct the captain of the corvette[1]
to attend to one (if they should separate) while he dealt with the
other, and as he had the First Lieutenant and a hundred of the
stoutest men in the ship ready to board her after the first broad-
side, he hoped very soon to be at liberty to go to the assistance of
the corvette.

Maitland added that it was probable that the emissaries were so
insistent because they felt themselves in danger from the French
side, notwithstanding that Rovigo had stated at the end of the
conversations that the Emperor had not exhausted his resources
and could still re-join his armies south of the Loire.

But everyone knew that it was too late. Maybe at Laon, had he
known that Grouchy was safe, Napoleon could have manœuvred,
as he had in 1814, between the English and Prussian armies
which had invaded that territory after Waterloo. At Laon, it
seemed, the Emperor had several chances to restore his position.
But after Laon all was lost. Savary's remark sprang solely from a
wish to impress the British.

Maitland asked to be excused for his disjointed letter and
explained that he was being badgered every moment by the two
Frenchmen, who kept raising new points, which had in fact
already been dealt with. He replied as follows to the letter of the
Grand Marshal:

Sir,
    I have to acknowledge the honour of your letter of yesterday's
date addressed to the Admiral Commanding the English Squadron
before Rochefort, acquainting me that the Emperor, having abdicated the Throne of France and chosen the United States of
America as an asylum, is now embarked on board the Frigates at
Rochefort to proceed for that destination, and awaits a passport
from the English Government, requesting to know if I have any
knowledge of such passports, and if I think it is the intention of the
English Government to prevent the Emperor's voyage.
    In reply I have the honour to acquaint you that I cannot say
what the intention of my Government may be; but the Countries
at present being in a State of War, I cannot allow any ship of War

[1] The *Daphne*

to be put to sea from the Port of Rochefort: as to the proposal
made by the Duke of Rovigo and the Count de Las Cases, of allow-
ing the Emperor to proceed in a Merchant Vessel, it is out of my
power without the sanction of my Commanding Officer (Sir Henry
Hotham) who is at present in Quiberon Bay, and to whom I have
forwarded your dispatch, to allow any Vessel under whatever flag
she may be to pass with a Personage of so much Consequence.

I have the honour to be,

F. L. MAITLAND
Captain of H.M. Ship *Bellerophon*.

Maitland's circumspection stands out. A simple ship's captain,
detached to Rochefort by his squadron commander, he was neither
disposed nor in a position to play a political role in a matter of such
importance. Maitland had his orders. He complied with them as
a disciplined officer should.

That is the English version of the first contacts on 10 July.
Captain Maitland has been criticized on the ground that wishing
to entice the Emperor on board his ship, he had let it be understood that England would admit him and treat him well, thus
clearly raising false hopes in his interlocutors. On this point
Captain Maitland, in his account written in 1825,[1] recalled that
after Savary had assured him of Napoleon's peaceful intentions,
he replied 'If that is the case, why shouldn't he ask for asylum in
England?' It is important to bear in mind that Maitland put this
reply in its right perspective, that is to say, the expression of a
personal opinion, and was at pains to repeat the terms of his letter
to Count Bertrand as set out above; in other words, not knowing
his Government's intentions, he could make no promises.

In short, the exploratory mission entrusted to Savary and Las
Cases was abortive. No safe-conducts to hope for; therefore, no
chance of going to America, and nothing definite from Maitland
as to the reception to be expected in England. Lallemand and
Planat de la Faye considered that their opposition to surrendering

[1] In his *Memorial of St Helena* Las Cases said, 'It was suggested we surrendered in England, where we were assured we had no reason to fear bad treatment'. Montholon, in his *Memoirs* says 'On the 10th, the British frigate prevented
Napoleon from sailing. He ordered Count de Las Cases to ask the British
Captain if he would permit him to sail for America. Captain Maitland replied
that he had no instructions in the matter, but he would receive Napoleon on
board and would take him to England if he wished. Napoleon attempted various
means of escape.'

to the English was vindicated. The *Bellerophon* had taken up a position in the Basque Roads such that the *Saale* and the *Méduse* were in her line of fire. A reconnaissance confirmed the fears entertained as to the fire power of the English warship.

Napoleon immediately decided to proceed to Aix and set himself up in the official residence he had built during a tour of inspection. His bedroom would be the large room on the ground floor, since it had four exits, an ever-present consideration when his security was increasingly threatened.

In this extremity, a few young naval officers proposed to take the Emperor and a few members of his staff out to sea on one of the coastal luggers, and then, with cutlasses between their teeth, to board the first merchant ship they encountered and compel her to set course for the United States. The initiative displayed by these bewildered youngsters is touching. But what chance had it of approval?

The brave Ponée offered to grapple the side of the *Bellerophon* while the *Saale* made good her escape. But Napoleon knew that Philibert would not take the responsibility for such an attempt, which would have been completely in violation of the formal orders he had received. It would also be too costly in human lives. He rejected the proposal. The timid Gourgaud now became almost offensive. He was against any escape that was discreditable or likely to cause bloodshed. At first opposed to surrender to the British, he seemed now to lean towards it.

The greatest confusion prevailed amongst the Emperor's staff. Discussions went on, plan succeeded plan without anyone getting anywhere. Each had his own point to make. There were clashes of opinion and the Emperor could not make up his mind which of the few courses open to him he should take. Lallemand, who had been sent on a secret mission to Bordeaux to make contact with Captain Baudin of the *Bayadère*, had returned to Aix. He reported that, although Baudin's chances had not improved in the last few days, he could slip through the sympathetic Becker's hands and reach the Gironde. In the end Napoleon rejected this plan, to consider again, by a curious change of view, an escape out to the open sea in a coastal craft. Some small vessels were actually brought and loaded with luggage. This last chance was still open. Becker presented himself to the Emperor to report that all was ready and that the captain was waiting, but he stressed that there must be no hesitation, otherwise the Emperor ran the risk of being at the mercy of Richard, a former member of the Convention, now appointed by his friend Fouché, prefect of Charente-Inférieure. Louis XVIII had just entered Paris. The fleur-de-lys was flying at Rochefort. Becker wanted to avoid the humiliation of witnessing the Emperor's arrest. Napoleon was about to settle for this desperate solution when he became aware of the disapproval of his entourage, the more important members of which had compromised themselves by following him and were apprehensive of the consequences of being left behind. Accordingly the Emperor changed his mind. So passed the opportune moment for a last attempt to escape. When King Joseph arrived at the last moment and proposed that Napoleon board a first class merchant ship about to sail for America (where she arrived safely)—or alternatively that he (Joseph) should pose at Aix as the Emperor —the fraternal offers were declined.

General Becker confirms that at this tragic juncture the Emperor's faithful band were disturbed at the thought of separation at their master's departure and that he was subjected to pressure by persons formerly in the inner counsels of the Empire to advise His Majesty to decide against precarious plans of escape and to throw himself on the generosity of the Prince Regent of Great Britain. He adds that the British people would doubtless be flattered at having in their country the noblest of their enemies and would welcome him with all the honour due to his name.

There was not the slightest doubt, though it is only to be inferred from what Becker says, that this suggestion came from Savary, and it may well have had its origin in the conversation between the former Minister of Police and Maitland, during which the latter, thinking aloud, used the words we have already mentioned, 'Why shouldn't Bonaparte ask for asylum in England?' Savary, remembering his misdeeds, had no illusion as to the fate that awaited him if he were arrested in France.[1] He had, therefore, the greatest interest in linking his future to Napoleon's, in not separating from him or letting himself be separated from him. In that case, the English solution had advantages for everyone and was the lesser evil. With the help of Las Cases, he held out bright

[1] Savary, as Chief of Police, was to a large extent responsible for the prompt execution of the Duc d'Enghien.

prospects of its success to the vacillating Emperor. And it was the better to persuade Napoleon that Savary had sought the support of General Becker, who himself wished to bring his painful mission to an early conclusion.

In the end, since Maitland had not been able to give either safe conduct or guarantees, the idea of an appeal over his head to the Prince Regent was the only one that could be considered in the present impasse. Furthermore, the idea of a message from one sovereign to another had a certain nobility, and would appeal to the Emperor. In the end the Emperor agreed.

So ended the most extraordinary vacillation, inexplicable in a man of decision like Napoleon, had we not evidence of these events in the reminiscences of General Becker. The fact is that at this period the Emperor was already a sick man, much more so than those close to him realized, for he had great mastery over physical pain and was adept at concealing it. It is only true to say that the cancer which was to carry him off six years later had long been secretly troubling him and he had (certainly since Elba, and perhaps since Moscow) been suffering from other complaints. His reverses, the severe blow to his morale caused by his defeat, the lack of medical care, all aggravated his condition.

General Becker was the closest witness of this sad state of affairs and his conclusions are worth reporting. Becker had been instructed not to leave the side of the Emperor; from the outset of his mission he had slept in the next room to Napoleon. On board the *Saale* only a linen curtain separated them, and the least sound or movement could be detected. Becker writes:

> The indecision evident at Rochfort and Malmaison was repeated on board the *Saale* and at Aix. This deterioration in energy and activity was not surprising, for the infirmities to which Napoleon had become subject were such as undermined strength of will and character. I often heard the groans caused by the painful condition which was already tormenting him at Waterloo. During that fateful day it prevented him from going about with his usual vigour to different parts of the field.

The condition was known as dysuria, which, in its acute form, manifests itself in a weakening of the will. General Becker's observation, then, is a vital one for understanding these events. A

sick man does not board a coastal craft with the same determination as a well man; a sick man is not fit to ride to the Gironde or
to put up with the frustrations of a man on the run.

Such were the straits in which Napoleon gathered his companions
together and told them of his decision to surrender to the English
fleet, but at the same time placing confidence, as Savary desired,
in the Prince Regent. Napoleon asked them for their views and they
were all in agreement, the remaining misgivings of Gourgaud and
Montholon having been overcome. The *Bellerophon* was the last
hope. They would join her at once. Nevertheless, Lallemand
intervened to press the Emperor to have regard solely to his own
interests before taking an irrevocable decision, and added that
although he might place confidence in Maitland, the Cabinet in
London might well overrule him. This observation, though a final
counsel of prudence, did not impress Napoleon. He had come to
realize the futility of the overtures to the English captain, and
summed up the situation in these words, as reported by Marchand:
'There is always a danger in trusting one's self to the enemy, but
there is less risk in trusting to his honour than in falling a legal
prisoner into his hands.'

In fact, once the plenipotentiaries had returned empty-handed,
he had committed to paper the terms of his appeal to the Prince
Regent, the only available avenue of escape — an appeal, furthermore, which would have been unnecessary if the negotiations
initiated with the captain of the *Bellerophon* had justified even a
slight hope — which shows that their character had been clearly
negative, and so untainted with any deception.

A fair copy having been made, apparently on the 13th, signed
and dated, the Imperial message was to have been taken next day
by Gourgaud, Las Cases and Lallemand to the *Bellerophon*.
Gourgaud was entrusted with the task of delivering it to the Prince
Regent through the proper channels without delay.

Actually, the next morning, the 14 July, the original message
was handed to Maitland and is today in the Royal archives at
Windsor. Furthermore, the authentic rough draft is extant,
containing the immortal words which impress with the seal of
greatness the final and humiliating act of a dazzling career, an act
that, understandably, cost the pride of the fallen Emperor so
much:

Rochefort, July 13th, 1815.

Your Royal Highness,

A victim to the factions which distract my country, and to the enmity of the greatest powers of Europe, I have terminated my political career, and I come, like Themistocles, to throw myself on the hospitality[1] of the British people. I put myself under the protection of their laws; which I claim from Your Royal Highness, as the most powerful, the most constant, and the most generous of my enemies.[2]

NAPOLEON.

The copies of this document had hardly been blotted when Maitland gave the order to the *Slaney* to get under way with Gourgaud, bearer of the Imperial message, on board, while he, Maitland, awaited the arrival of Napoleon. Maitland, in addition, entrusted to the *Slaney* the following letter:

Basque Roads 14 July, 1815.

To the Secretary of the Admiralty,

14th July, 1815.

Sir,

For the information of the Lords Commissioners of the Admiralty, I have to acquaint you that the Count Las Cases and General Lallemand this day came on board His Majesty's ship under my command, with a proposal from Count Bertrand for me to receive on board Napoleon Buonaparte, for the purpose of throwing himself on the generosity of the Prince Regent. Conceiving myself authorised by their Lordships' secret order, I have acceded to the proposal, and he is to embark on board this ship tomorrow morning.[3] That no misunderstanding might arise, I have

[1] Napoleon, in the original, had first written 'on the ashes', which is a close translation from the Greek of Plutarch.

[2] This note was also appended by Gourgaud: 'A rough draft, written in full in his own hand by the Emperor Napoleon, of the letter which he had despatched me to bear from the Île d'Aix to the Prince Regent of England on 14 July, 1815.'

Island of St Helena,

Gourgaud, *Baron, General of Artillery.*

At St Helena the Emperor gave this historic document as a present to Gourgaud with a marginal note: 'To Gourgaud, General of Artillery, *Napoleon.*'

[3] In fact, Napoleon presented himself at dawn on the 16th. In the *Memorial of Saint Helena* Las Cases says of the 14th July 'I returned at four a.m. with General Lallemand aboard the *Bellerophon* to find out if any message had arrived. The English Captain told us that he was expecting it at any moment, and added that if the Emperor wished to embark immediately for England, he was authorised to receive him on board and conduct him thither. He went on to say that in his private opinion, in which he was joined by several of the other Captains present, he had never doubted but that Napoleon would find in England all the distinguished treatment he could wish.'

explicitly and clearly explained to Count de Las Cases that I have no authority whatever for granting terms of any sort, but that all I can do is to carry him and his suite to England, to be received in such manner as His Royal Highness may deem expedient.

At Napoleon Buonaparte's request, and that their Lordships may be in possession of the transaction at as early a period as possible, I despatch the *Slaney* (with General Gourgaud, his Aide de Camp), directing Captain Sartorius to put into the nearest port, and forward this letter by his first Lieutenant, and shall in compliance with their Lordships' orders proceed to Torbay, and to await such directions as the Admiralty may think proper to give.

Enclosed, I transmit a copy of the letter with which General Gourgaud is charged to his Royal Highness the Prince Regent, and request that you will acquaint their Lordships that the General informs me, he is entrusted with further particulars, which he is anxious to communicate to His Royal Highness.

I am, Sir, etc.

F. MAITLAND.

These messages were summarized in an *aide-mémoire* in which the Emperor stated that Gourgaud, on arrival in England, was to seek an audience of the Prince Regent and to present the following stipulations:

If H.R.H. sees no objection to granting me passports to go to the United States, it would be my intention to go there. But I do not desire to go to any other colony. If I cannot go to America, I wish to stay in England, assuming the name of Muiron[1] or Duroc.[2] In England I would like to live in a country house about ten to twelve leagues from London, after arriving strictly incognito. I would need a house large enough for my staff. I ask to keep away from London where I do not think the Government would like me to live. If the Government intends to provide me with a superintendent, he must not be a jailer but a man of quality and honour.

How could the Emperor imagine that these demands would be favourably received?

Meanwhile, one thing must be told to complete the story. On 15 July Las Cases delivered a note to Captain Maitland from Marshal Bertrand informing him that next day, before dawn, the Emperor would present himself at the gangway of the *Bellerophon,* either to be given the safe-conducts to enable him to proceed to

---

[1] The officer who, at Arcole, had shielded him with his body.
[2] A school and life-long friend of Napoleon, killed at Lutzen in 1813.

America or, if that were not possible, to be conveyed to England, where he wished to reside as a private citizen. No formal document was annexed to the letter.

Later, Captain Maitland was to write in his book that the opinion he then expressed — that it was impossible for him to give any undertaking as to the treatment Napoleon would receive on reaching English waters — would better have been committed to writing in view of the controversy that later developed. But as it was expressed in the presence of witnesses[1] it never occurred to him that such a formality would be necessary. Furthermore the best evidence that no agreement was made regarding Bonaparte's reception in England was that nothing was signed, which would certainly have been the case if, at the request of M. Las Cases, he had agreed to specific conditions.

Later, Captain Maitland wrote this letter, dated 18 July, to Lord Keith:[2]

Having received directions from Sir Henry Hotham to forward the accompanying despatch to Your Lordship by an officer, I avail myself of the opportunity to explain the circumstances under which I was placed when induced to receive Napoleon Buonaparte into the Ship I command.

After the first communication was made to me by Count Bertrand (a copy of which, with my answer, has been forwarded to Your Lordship by Sir Henry Hotham) that Buonaparte was at the Isle d'Aix, and actually embarked on board the Frigates for the purpose of proceeding to the United States of America, my duty became peculiarly difficult and anxious from the numerous reports that were daily brought from all quarters of his intention to escape in Vessels of various descriptions and from different situations on the Coast, which the limited means I possessed, together with the length of time requisite to communicate with Sir Henry Hotham at Quiberon Bay, rendered the success of (sic) at least possible and even probable.

Thus situated, the Enemy, having at least two Frigates and a Brig, while the force under my command consisted of the *Bellerophon* and *Slaney* (having detached the *Myrmidon* to reinforce the

---

[1] To wit: Savary, Las Cases, Lallemand, Gourgaud on the French side; Captain Sartorius in command of the *Slaney*, Captain Gambier, in command of the *Myrmidon* on the English side.

[2] This report was supplemented the following month before the departure of Napoleon for St Helena by a more detailed one on the direct instructions of Lord Keith.

Daphne off the Maumusson passage, where the force was consider-
ably superior to her, and whence one of the reports stated Buonaparte meant to sail) another Flag of Truce was sent out for the
ostensible reason of enquiring whether I had an answer to the
former, but I soon ascertained the real one to be a proposal from
Buonaparte to embark for England in this Ship. Taking into
consideration all the circumstances of the probability of the escape
being effected if the trial was made either in the Frigates or
clandestinely in a small vessel, as had this ship been disabled in
action, there was no other with me that could produce any effect on
a Frigate, and, from the experience I have had in blockading the
ports of the Bay, knowing the impossibility of preventing small
Vessels from putting to Sea, and looking upon it as of the greatest
importance to getting possession of Buonaparte, I was induced
without hesitation to accede to the proposal as far as taking him
on board and proceeding with him to England: but at the same
time stating in the most clear and positive terms, that I had no
authority to make any sort of stipulation as to the reception he was
to meet with.

Under all the circumstances I am happy to say the measures I
have adopted have met with the approbation of Sir Henry Hotham,
and will I trust and hope meet with that of Your Lordship, as
well as of His Majesty's Government.

I have the honour to be,
F. L. MAITLAND
Captain.

At dawn on the 16th the Emperor put on his favourite uniform,
that of Colonel of the Chasseurs de la Garde. In attendance were
his faithful staff, his Grand Marshal, his Aides-de-Camp, all in
uniform, with their wives and servants, in all about seventy people.
He embraced General Becker and saluted the sailors of Aix as he
had saluted the old soldiers at Fontainebleau. He boarded the
Épervier, a small vessel, to take him and his party and the baggage,
to the *Bellerophon*. As the *Épervier* made little headway through
lack of wind, Maitland became impatient and sent out a boat to
which the Emperor transferred. Soon after he set foot on board
Bellerophon. He was received with full honours, despite the fact
that in the Royal Navy honours are not paid between sunset and
sunrise.[1] His first words to Captain Maitland were: 'I come to put

---

[1] This is still the rule. Against standing orders, Maitland drew up the guard
on the foc'sle, and he and his officers received the Emperor bareheaded. In his

myself under the protection of your Prince and your laws.' As
General Becker wrote, his companions did not doubt that
England's welcome would be worthy of the rank of the man asking
for asylum and of the great nation from whom this modern Themistocles sought hospitality.

In short, Napoleon did not leave France as a fugitive but as an
Emperor, placing his entire confidence in the outcome of the most
hazardous of surrenders, and left the stage set for history and the
picture-books of Épinal; and this with the sure touch of a man who
had read his Plutarch, had applauded Talma, and had ordered his
own coronation.

Meanwhile, the *Superb*, living up to her name, had arrived at
full speed, and had hardly dropped anchor when Admiral Hotham
hastened in his barge to *Bellerophon*. A clever, plausible man, he
wished to snatch the Emperor from Maitland and reap the reward
of transporting him to England. But his subordinate, relying
apparently on some regulation, refused to hand him over. Also
Napoleon felt he had been well received in the *Bellerophon,* and
was not anxious to change. However, he agreed to dine in the
flagship on 17 July, and he was received by the Admiral with full
military honours. The sailors manned the yards and the French
were surprised by the quality of the food. As soon as the Emperor
had returned on board, the *Bellerophon* sailed for England.

It was not before time. On 13 July the new Minister of Marine,
the Comte de Jaucourt, despatched to Captain Philibert, on whose
ship Louis XVIII's government believed Napoleon to be, the
following orders supplementary to those already given to Richard,
the Prefect:

> Napoleon Bonaparte, who is on board the frigate under your
> command, is there merely as a prisoner whom all the sovereigns of
> Europe have a right to take. The King is not alone in claiming him.
> It is no longer possible for him to be governed by his natural
> generosity. The King of France, in pursuing Napoleon, is not
> acting in isolation and for his own private reasons. His cause is
> Europe's, just as the cause of Europe, in arms against Napoleon, is
> his. All forces attacking Napoleon Bonaparte attack in the name of

---

book Maitland wrote that, in the absence of guidance from the Admiralty as to
the compliments to be paid to Napoleon in the event of his capture, he had been
happy to overlook that the Emperor had arrived before 8 a.m.

the King. Consequently, Frenchmen who do not wish to be regarded as rebels against their king and country must regard as Allies and friends the commanders by land and sea whose objective, if circumstances permit, is the capture of Napoleon. I must, therefore, point out to you that the commander of the English naval forces blockading Rochefort is authorized to require the captain of the frigate in which Napoleon is embarked to return him immediately. This notice will not be given in the name of His Britannic Majesty alone; it will be given in the name of the King, your legitimate sovereign. You should not consider as a purely English officer the officer commanding the English naval force who may serve you with the present order. He is under the orders of the King of France. I therefore direct that you hand over Napoleon Bonaparte to the English commander, who will claim him. If you were so misguided as to resist my instructions, you would be in overt rebellion and would be responsible for any bloodshed resulting from the destruction of your ship.

When the letter arrived the *Bellerophon* was already making her way to England. At least the Emperor had been spared the indignity of being arrested.

CHAPTER 3

The Status of the Prisoner

But victory had not taught them magnanimity. They were honest men acting up to their lights: we can only regret that the men were dull and the lights were dim.

LORD ROSEBERY

THE NEWS of the victory of Waterloo, which the house of Rothschild were the first to hear, caused an outburst of joy in London and was an immense relief to England. The British policy of holding on had paid. The action of its champion, Pitt, and later of Lord Liverpool, Prime Minister since 1812 and an extreme Tory, was justified. The war was over; it had ended in a sudden and marvellous fashion, unlooked for by the Allies. Further news reached London a month later. The Emperor, urged towards Rochefort by Fouché, and lacking the safe-conducts this scoundrel had promised, had been compelled to rely on the discretion of the English; he was their prisoner. An unexpected and unprecedented situation arose. It fell to the British Cabinet to settle his fate, not only as a defeated person and a captive, but to determine his status, to decide upon the measures to be taken in his case; all most delicate problems requiring careful thought.

Lord Liverpool was a gifted man, no mean orator, and a Prime Minister who at a particularly difficult time had succeeded in keeping his Cabinet together. On the other hand, he was a hard man who governed harshly. He had introduced a measure directed against Queen Caroline which was unconstitutional in its object. The war had compelled him to increase taxation, and in levying it he had not hesitated to resort to the most brutal and unpopular measures. Such a man was not going to be too particular about Napoleon. To him Bonaparte was the Corsican Ogre, the murderer of the Duc d'Enghien and Captain Wright,[1] the man

---

[1] John Wesley Wright (1769–1805) an Irish sailor was a friend of the famous Admiral Sir Sydney Smith. First arrested for plotting against France, he

who had deprived legitimate kings of their thrones, caused the deaths of millions of men, someone to be hated, a scourge of humanity.

Nor would Government circles be likely to take a more merciful view. As Lord Rosebery bluntly put it, neither Lord Liverpool nor his Cabinet colleagues were supermen. Nevertheless the successors of Pitt, Castlereagh in particular, had inherited his vital spark. They were conscious of holding in their hands the fate of their country and of the world, and being aware of this, they devoted all their energy and obstinacy to their task. They were engaged in a fight to a finish; they had succeeded in holding their own against Napoleon—and that at a time when the Crown was worn by an insane King and the Regent was dissolute (though for all that resolute). They had succeeded in holding their own by maintaining an immense fleet in action, defying invasion and resisting a Continental blockade, by fitting out large expeditionary forces to Walcheren and the Peninsula, maintaining coalitions, intensifying diplomacy, distributing subsidies to the Allies, and suffering cruel losses; whilst at home business was at a standstill, and the City in despair.

The wars against the Empire had cost England more than a thousand million pounds sterling. On the eve of Waterloo Consols had fallen to 42. After suffering the severest trials and the see-sawings of fortune, after resisting the violent attacks of a liberal opposition (which, inspired by Samuel Whitbread,[1] a disciple of Fox, advocated a negotiated peace) these men had emerged victorious. More than that, the mighty genius, who since the turn of the century had directed against their country the most dangerous war machine of all time, had fallen into their power. What chance was there that these men after such trials would give

---

succeeded in escaping from the Temple. In 1804, after landing Georges Cadoudal on the Norman coast he was taken to the Ile d'Houat and again imprisoned in the Temple, where one morning he was, like Pichegru, found dead in his cell. The English government accused the Imperial government of having liquidated him.

[1] Samuel Whitbread (1759–1815) wealthy proprietor of the brewery of the same name, a member of the 'aristocracy without title' and through family connections one of the most formidable of Pitt's opponents. Struggled hard at first to avoid the war against the Republic, and favoured peace during the Napoleonic period. He fought in vain against the ruthless treatment of France by the Allies. Succeeded Fox as the leader of the Whig party. Committed suicide a few days after Waterloo.

way to humanitarian impulses? None. Victory would not teach them magnanimity. They were strangers to such a feeling. At the end of a bloody struggle they would make the most of their advantage. Lord Liverpool's Foreign Secretary, Lord Castlereagh —who, in consequence of an attack brought on by the immense strains he had been under, was to cut his throat with a penknife a few years later—had reluctantly signed the Treaty of Fontainebleau.

With such men in the Cabinet room in Downing Street sat Melville,[1] First Lord of the Admiralty and friend of Pitt; Lord Bathurst,[2] Secretary of State for War and the Colonies, a hardhearted man, blinded by hatred of France and Napoleon, who was to act for the Government in all matters relating to Napoleon, and who would not hesitate to take extreme measures. He was to appoint Hudson Lowe as Governor of St Helena. There was also Lord Vansittart, Chancellor of the Exchequer. All these men were firmly resolved to put Napoleon in a position where he would be harmless. They felt themselves answerable to posterity for the fate of a man whose existence was the greatest disgrace of modern times. These ministers, in addition, had the support of a colleague of high calibre, the Lord Chancellor of England.

The presence of the Lord Chancellor in the Cabinet always strikes the puzzled foreigner as a particular anomaly of the British political system. The origins of his exalted office are complex. Originally he was an ecclesiastic of high rank like Thomas à Becket, Archbishop of Canterbury, chaplain to the king and 'Keeper of the King's conscience'. As such he became the judge, on the king's behalf, of petitions from subjects aggrieved at the strict and harsh decisions of the Common Law courts. He gave judgement, not according to law, but according to the rules of Equity and being a court of last resort it became the final court of appeal for the Kingdom, that is, he exercised what is now the jurisdiction of the

[1] Robert Dundas, Lord Melville. First Lord of the Admiralty from 1812 to 1827, and from 1828 to 1830. Pioneer of Arctic exploration, the straits and islands of Melville were named after him.

[2] Henry, Earl Bathurst (1762–1836) a member of an old family tracing its origins to the Norman Conquest. Son of a retired Lord Chancellor, President of the Board of Trade and Master of the Mint in 1804. Secretary of State for War and the Colonies from 1812 to 1828, in which year Lord Liverpool's Government fell. Lord President of the Council in Wellington's administration from 1828 to 1830.

House of Lords. From that, it was only one step to presiding over the House of Lords, a political assembly; and that step he took. Then because of his special knowledge he found himself involved in the counsels of ministers, i.e. the Cabinet. By the time of Napoleon the three-fold role of the Lord Chancellor was well established.

If the Lord Chancellor of the day was not a dominant personality he did not play an important part in the deliberations of Government. He confined himself to his functions as Speaker of the House of Lords and President of the highest court of the United Kingdom. If, on the other hand, the Lord Chancellor was a man of great ability his membership of the Cabinet conferred great importance on him. He actively participated in its work and, if he were a political as well as a judicial leader, he could bring his two-fold influence to bear on its decisions. Indeed, in Napoleon's case, it was the views of the Lord Chancellor which prevailed. The Lord Chancellor was the famous Lord Eldon,[1] whose career, although it began with a runaway marriage at Gretna Green, had been brilliant, and he had been the trusted counsellor of successive governments. A great lawyer, he knew all there was to know of English law, but was not always at home with international law, a field he had left to his brother, Sir William Scott,[2] a lawyer who had also reached the top of his profession. Lord Eldon, in spite of his outstanding qualities and vast knowledge, was both harsh and narrow-minded as evidenced in his implacable opposition to Catholic Emancipation. He was as incapable of indulgence towards Napoleon as Lord Liverpool's colleagues.

Without doubt, Napoleon's case, considering all the circumstances including his embarkation in the *Bellerophon,* was exceptional. First, in what capacity was the Emperor to be received? That was the first thing for the Cabinet to decide. Was Napoleon a prisoner

---

[1] John Scott, Viscount Encombe, Earl of Eldon (1751–1838). Called to the Bar in 1776. Elected to the House of Commons in 1782. Solicitor-General in 1788, raised to the peerage and appointed Lord Chancellor in 1801. He acquired great influence in parliamentary circles. By contributing to the fall of Lord Addington in 1804, he facilitated the return of Pitt to power. Resigning in 1806, he became Lord Chancellor again in the following year and continued to hold office until 1827.

[2] Sir William Scott (1745–1838). After being called to the Bar became a specialist in civil, maritime and international law. Famous for his wit and culture. M.P. for Downton and then the University of Oxford. President of the Admiralty Court, 1798. Created Baron Stowell in 1821.

4

and a sovereign, like Jean le Bon,[1] for example, who spent many years in England, captive not only of his victor, Edward III, but of his mistresses? No, because Napoleon could not be the object of ransom. No, because Napoleon had been forced to abdicate. No, because strictly speaking, he had never been recognized as Emperor by His Majesty's Government. In its eyes, Napoleon had never been more than First Consul. Admittedly, the British Government had recognized him as such, but Bonaparte had resigned that office to place on his own head the Imperial crown.[2] Now, Napoleon, having violated the Treaty of Fontainebleau by his escape from Elba, and so lost any right to be treated as a sovereign, could only be regarded by the British Government as a General, having been a Commander-in-Chief, and that was how the prisoner on board the *Bellerophon* would be treated. And as he had lost his status as a sovereign, honours and compliments to be paid would be no greater than those appropriate to that rank – as the First Lord of the Admiralty was to instruct Lord Keith, commanding the naval base at Plymouth and the Channel and Eastern Atlantic Squadron.

But this question of title was only a secondary one. The chief point was that Napoleon was in British hands and it was important to determine the nature and legality of his detention. Was it arbitrary? No, since no one could establish its illegality. He had voluntarily come on board the *Bellerophon* without any under-taking by her captain as to the consequences of his surrender. Las Cases had unsuccessfully attempted to attach conditions to it; they were of no weight and attracted no rights in return. The difficulty, as the Cabinet quite rightly saw it, was that Napoleon had not been taken prisoner while waging war. No truce or armistice having been reached with him since his escape from Elba, he had to be regarded as a prisoner of war. Napoleon was such, both 'de facto' and 'de jure'. But if he was to be treated as a prisoner of war, he should, in accordance with international law, be set free on the

---

[1] Jean le Bon, born in 1319, died in the Tower of London in 1364. It was he who, having paid his ransom and been released from his first imprisonment, returned to London to take the place of his son who, when a hostage, had broken his parole. Said the father, 'If good faith were banished from the rest of the earth, yet it should have a place in the heart of a king.'

[2] Nevertheless, England had addressed Napoleon as Emperor during negotiations with him in Paris in 1806 carried out by the mission headed by Lord Lauderdale, and at Châtillon by that of Lord Castlereagh.

conclusion of a treaty of peace, which was just what the Government did not want to do. As to the laws of hospitality, how could Napoleon take advantage of them? By his request to the Prince Regent, Napoleon purported to expunge immediately twenty years of 'blood, toil, tears and sweat', to quote a later phrase, that he had cost the British; he assumed that the 'nation of shopkeepers', as he had so often called it, would welcome him with open arms. It was a lot to ask. However, the British Government, though Napoleon was anxious to give himself up to it, could have got rid of him. Lord Liverpool had written in a letter to Lord Castlereagh: 'The easiest course would be to deliver him up to the King of France who might try him as a rebel, but then we must be quite certain that he must be tried in such a manner as to have no chance of escape.'

In such an eventuality, however, the Emperor would be exposed to the most cruel of fates, indeed might well be shot, since Louis XVIII, who at the close of the year 1815 was to refuse to pardon Ney, would be unlikely to show any mercy to Napoleon and would be obliged to comply with the relentless decision of the Allies spurred on by Blücher. Wellington, on being consulted, despite criticism from extremists in both countries, intervened and persuaded the Prime Minister that it was better to retain Napoleon in the power of Great Britain. Furthermore, Louis XVIII could easily have arrested Napoleon at Aix if Fouché had shown the least diligence. The latter was probably reluctant to do so, preferring to see the fugitive caught in the English net. The advice of Wellington prevailed. The Emperor would not be surrendered to the Allies.

If Napoleon was not a sovereign, if his person were denied the protection of English law, if England refused him hospitality, if she deemed it inexpedient to hand him over to the Allies for them to proceed against him according to their law, what authority had they to detain the imprudent man who had offered his person to the *Bellerophon*? Could one pretend that he was no more nor less than an outlaw as the great jurist Bracton[1] described him: 'a man whose life was in the king's hands', who could deal with him as he saw fit to safeguard his people against the hostile return of a dangerous person.

[1] Henry de Bracton (1200–1268) famous theologian whose work, *De legibus et consuetudinibus Angliae* still retains its authority. A great judge under Henry III. He invented the constitutional maxim: 'The King reigns under God and the law.'

These important questions continued to preoccupy the British Cabinet which, in accordance with custom, turned to the Lord Chancellor for advice. Himself a prey to many doubts, Lord Eldon decided to consult the highest legal talents in the country: Lord Ellenborough,[1] Sir William Grant, Master of the Rolls,[2] the Attorney-General, the Solicitor-General, the two Law Officers of the Crown, and his own brother.

There has been preserved in the British archives a long fragment of an undated letter, probably written at the end of July, in which Lord Eldon, after consultation and reflection, wrote to Scott, seemingly, to clarify his own ideas. It is revealing. The document is very long and involved; its manner resembles those of the writs drawn up by its author, who was not a man of letters, but the power of its thought stands out. It may reasonably be inferred that the man behind the Cabinet decisions was certainly the Lord Chancellor who, as a good lawyer, at any rate in Frederick II's sense of the term, gives what he considers adequate reasons for his decisions — at any rate in the short term.

Lord Eldon began by referring to the opinions he had obtained from Lord Ellenborough and Sir William Scott. He went on to say that,

> According to Lord Ellenborough a state of war might have existed not only between two Powers, but also between one Power and any one person on his own who might be the subject of another Power: from which it would follow that the peace reached with France could have excluded any settlement with Napoleon personally and would have classified him as an enemy alien who could be interned as such.
>
> According to Sir William Scott, as far as England is concerned, Napoleon's status is that of a prisoner of war. In so far as he is a French subject he is only responsible to the French Government

---

[1] Edward Law, first Baron Ellenborough (1750–1818), son of an Anglican bishop and brother of two more. Called to the Bar in 1780, he defended Warren Hastings and after seven years' effort secured his acquittal. Chief Justice in 1802, in which year he was raised to the peerage. Opposed to any mitigation of the criminal law, particularly of the death penalty for theft. Noted for his profound knowledge of the law, but also for his severity.

[2] Sir William Grant (1755–1822). Called to the Bar in 1774, he went to Canada where he soon became Attorney-General. Returning to London he was noticed by Pitt who assisted his advancement. Member of Parliament, 1790. A good speaker, he was admired for his logic and command of language. Appointed Master of the Rolls in 1800.

for his illegal actions. They concern the French Government alone, since it possesses the sovereign power, and is responsible for these actions as far as other nations are concerned. According to the laws of nations, peace with a sovereign means peace with all his subjects. Subjects cannot be at war while their sovereign is at peace. But a subject may rebel against his sovereign and then that sovereign's allies must help him to put down the rebellion.

Sir William Scott was familiar with the classic doctrine of international law which his opinion reflects. Lord Eldon then delivers himself of his own thoughts, which may be summarized thus:

1. Lord Ellenborough and Sir William Scott hold Napoleon to be a French subject and take the same stand whether England is at war with France, or whether Napoleon is in fact a rebel, and England France's ally. In either case— given that one or other is correct— the British Government has not *so far* taken any questionable action. That a state of war exists between Britain and France is well known to the British Parliament—no peace treaty has yet ended it. Therefore, for the time being, there is no reason why Napoleon should not be detained as a prisoner of war. According to the report of the Captain of *Bellerophon,* Napoleon was aware of the sentiments of the British Government when he gave himself up, and no undertakings had been entered into with him.

2. Nevertheless, had England been at war with France at the time? Lord Eldon was inclined to think that she had only been at war with Napoleon and his supporters, and that she had not been allied to the Bourbons. France could choose whatever government she liked, Bourbon or otherwise, so long as she rejected Bonaparte.

3. Bonaparte was no longer a French subject since his abdication as Emperor of the French: he had become King of Elba. During the Hundred Days the Allies had never thought of him as a French subject, and certainly not as a rebel against the French Government. As a consequence, if Napoleon was neither a French subject nor a rebel, he could be disassociated from France altogether. He had been defeated in a legitimate war fought *against himself.* It was therefore lawful for the British Government to treat him as a prisoner of war as long as was necessary and thus they would avoid any danger he might cause if set at liberty.

4. An Act of Indemnity protected ministers from any proceedings in the British courts, but afforded them none in international law, since Napoleon was not a British subject.

5. Finally, the principal reason, as Lord Eldon saw it, was that policy and the safety of the world, jointly charged him to detain

Napoleon *sine die*, since this was the only way to prevent any future trouble. Moreover, Napoleon could only be regarded as an adventurer, a vagabond, one of those men described by Vattel,[1] 'who do not feel bound by any treaty.'

The concluding part of this document has been lost or destroyed. Even so, it is sufficient to bring out the considerations on which the British Cabinet based their decision in regard to Napoleon's fate. It has been thought that the decisions were motivated by purely diplomatic and political considerations. That was not so. Certainly diplomacy, under Lord Castlereagh's leadership played a great part in these events and, for its part, the British Cabinet, on the whole, applied itself to a problem described by Lord Liverpool as 'one of the thorniest'. It certainly called in, and listened to, the highest legal luminaries in the Kingdom, in particular Lord Chancellor Eldon who, though less learned in international law than some others, could isolate the issues and define the captive's position and give, so far as was possible, a juridical basis for the Government's action.

Napoleon having been, provisionally at any rate, classed as a prisoner of war, the next question was to decide where he was to be detained. A comprehensive solution was imperative, particularly as the Allies had been badly deceived when they imagined twelve months ago, that Napoleon would be satisfied with his Kingdom of Elba; and also because they were dealing with a man formidable in capacity and drive, still in the prime of life at 46 (no one guessed the seriousness of the complaint which was even then attacking him), at the peak of his intellectual powers, whose superior strategy would have triumphed in Flanders had he had subordinates worthy of him. Would it be necessary for the sake of everyone's security, to put Napoleon in chains, as Caesar had in the case of Vercingetorix, to throw him *'in carcere duro'*, as many potentates had done with their prisoners? Should they place him in a cage like Cardinal La Balue or cast him into some Bastille like Latude? Could he be imprisoned in the Tower of London or Sheerness

---

[1] Emerich de Vattel (1714–1767), diplomat; he represented the Elector of Saxony at Berne, subsequently entering the service of the Cabinet at Dresden. Author of a book well known at the time, *The Rights of Man or the Principles of Natural Law applied to the Conduct of the Affairs of Nations and Sovereigns.*

Castle, or banished to a Scottish castle, where later his ghost might prowl, the moor and heather forming a screen between him and the rest of the world? The latter was a solution proposed by Lord Castlereagh, who thought it would be useful to have Napoleon at home during the peace negotiations, and one to which Metternich inclined, for was not Napoleon his sovereign's son-in-law? No, they would have to look for somewhere distant — the northern hemisphere was ruled out — some convenient place in the southern hemisphere where Napoleon would be kept forcibly in permanent residence, preferably an island, since surveillance of an island, provided the nearest coast is distant, is the easiest for a country having command of the sea.

Now there happened to be an island which would meet the required conditions, the name of which was already in mind and towards which the British Cabinet was attracted. Wellington had already suggested it as an alternative to surrendering Napoleon to the Allies, an alternative which, apart from anything else, would have been disgraceful in the eyes of the British people, and which Wellington had the wisdom to reject. While serving in India, Arthur Wellesley, as he was then known, had put in at St Helena and had explored the little island on horseback. It belonged to the East India Company,[1] who, after taking it over from the Dutch, the original occupiers, turned it into a port of call for ships rounding the Cape of Good Hope, despite the fact that the Cape was 1,000 sea miles away. But that was before the days of steam, when ships were at the mercy of the winds, and were sometimes blown off course. The nearest land was Ascension Island, 800 miles away. Bordered by high cliffs, St Helena's only landing place was the port of Jamestown. From a peak 2,500 feet high, days being normally clear, any approaching vessel could be seen at a very great distance.

Did not a place so remote and with such advantages exactly meet the requirements? In addition, the climate of this place was pleasant enough, according to travellers, not the least of whom was

[1] The East India Company which was imitated in France, but with less success by the Compagnie des Indes, was founded in the reign of Elizabeth I by English merchants, who obtained a Royal Charter. A century later, the East India Company was granted a monopoly of trade with India. Thereafter its position was paramount, and its activities were identified with British policy in India. Only in 1858 after the Mutiny was the Company taken over by the Crown.

Bory de Saint-Vincent,[1] who in 1802 had been there on a Government mission. St Helena was the 'little island' which by some curious premonition the cadet of Brienne[2] had entered in his geography note book. A further point was that the island belonged, not to the Crown, but to a chartered company: someone banished there would not, strictly speaking, be on British soil, and so would be outside the jurisdiction of the British Courts and therefore not in a position to avail himself of *Habeas Corpus*.

Having carefully considered the case, the Cabinet was to settle for St Helena, and in doing so it did not think it was showing excessive severity to one against whom the most serious indictment could be preferred. Rather it was thought of as a security measure. The great thing was that Napoleon would be permanently off the world stage. In return, he would have the advantage of not being surrendered to the Allies, or arraigned before a council of war, so saving his life and preserving him from the fate of rotting in a fortress. He would have fresh air, room for his activities, he could ride within fixed bounds, have a measure of liberty locally, and companions. The Cabinet, thinking of the successful mission of Colonel Campbell at Elba (though he had allowed his prisoner to escape!) could not foresee the disastrous appointment of Sir Hudson Lowe, and the gloomy consequences of the differences between Napoleon and his jailor.

Bonaparte would therefore go to St Helena. That was the decision which the British Government, as a matter of urgency, was going to take, a decision based on the necessity of self-preservation and of legitimate self-defence.

Was this decision in accordance with the fundamental law of the realm and of the higher law of morality binding civilized nations together. A law which a nation as civilized as England could not contravene without incurring a measure of blame, if not of remorse? There was some doubt. In any case, whilst the British Government decided to act with great despatch, it took the

---

[1] Jean-Baptiste Marie Georges Bory de Saint-Vincent (1780–1846). Soldier and naturalist, in 1802 took part in a scientific expedition under Captain Baudin. Later served in the principal campaigns under the Empire and reached the rank of general. In his *Voyage dans îles quatre principales îles des mers d'Afrique* he describes his passage to St Helena, where he put in without penetrating the interior of the island. He described it as volcanic and forbidding, but with a climate said to be very healthy.

[2] Napoleon Bonaparte.

precaution of obtaining an Act of Indemnity when Parliament re-assembled. It did so, on Lord Eldon's advice, to cover itself, since as far as English common law was concerned, the Act would be a ratification of its action.

Such were the decisions of the Government in London. It remained to implement them.

CHAPTER 4

In English Waters

This is one of the cornerstones of English law, the
bulwark of the nation's liberty.

VOLTAIRE

As WE HAVE SEEN, the order to the captain of the *Bellerophon*, should he manage to intercept Napoleon, was to take him to the nearest English port and there await further instructions. Captain Maitland had no knowledge of the ultimate fate of the Emperor. Neither did he know how the Prince Regent would react to the request addressed to him. Captain Maitland took the view, and rightly, that his mission did not preclude the paying of respects — and he, his officers and ship's company, entertained the greatest respect for the illustrious prisoner whom fate had cast in their path — he could make the Emperor welcome on board his ship which then became the envy of the Royal Navy. Napoleon — who had pleasant memories of the attentions he had enjoyed on board the *Undaunted*, the British frigate which had taken him to Elba — sat at the head of the Captain's table, had the freedom of the quarterdeck, took an interest in the working of ship and her discipline, and talked to the sailors. The swell did not worry him: it was like a rocking-chair which lulled him to dream that he would find in England the resting place he longed for. The atmosphere bred optimism. The members of his staff were the victims of some strange illusions. They saw themselves and their master comfortably installed in a manor-house in the country, enjoying the deference of the locals. Why should the Prince Regent not act like a kind prince? And if England could not be a jumping-off place for America, at least it would be a refuge and shelter from the wrath of the Allies.

On 24 July the lookout reported the grey of the English coast. Before long the *Bellerophon* was dropping anchor in Torbay, just south of Torquay in Devon. Napoleon assumed he would disembark within the hour. He was mistaken. This disappointment was

58

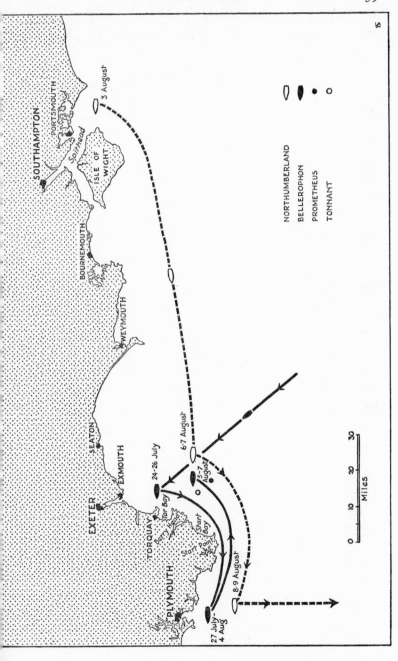

3 August

SOUTHAMPTON
PORTSMOUTH
Spithead
ISLE OF WIGHT
BOURNEMOUTH
WEYMOUTH
SEATON
EXETER
EXMOUTH
24-26 July
6-7 August
TORQUAY
Tor Bay
Berry Head
Start Bay
Start Point
PLYMOUTH
27 July-4 Aug
8-9 August
5-7 August

NORTHUMBERLAND
BELLEROPHON
PROMETHEUS
TONNANT

Miles
0   10   20   30

to be even more bitter when he saw the newspapers. The majority of these were mouthpieces of the Government and unmistakably hostile to him.

To give but one example: *The Times* fulminated against 'the most infamous of criminals'. Only Gourgaud, the bearer of the letter to the Prince Regent, who had arrived a few days before in the *Slaney,* was allowed ashore, though he was not allowed to go as far as London. He had to hand over his letter to an English messenger, and was compelled to return to the *Bellerophon.* General Lallemand, who had had misgivings about going to England, became increasingly apprehensive. The Emperor affected an attitude of patience.

In Torbay the *Bellerophon* became the object of general curiosity. She was surrounded by dozens of boats full of people of all classes wanting to get a glimpse of the Emperor. The crowd became troublesome. Captain Maitland had become a hero too. When his wife came out in a pinnace, she tried to attract his attention by making signals to him, while at the same time Napoleon, to whom someone had pointed her out, doffed his hat to her in salute. Lord Keith did not approve of all this hubbub and ordered *Bellerophon* to move further away. This movement was not understood by the French and the Emperor was disturbed. In his impatience he asked Captain Maitland to ask Lord Keith, the senior officer present who flew his flag in *Tonnant,* to confer with him. Lord Keith stalled; he had no instructions. The Emperor repeated his request next day. He was anxious about his letter to the Prince Regent. It had indeed been sent to London, but there was no information as to any further developments.

Meanwhile Lord Keith had been authorized to approach the Emperor. The latter discovered that the family name of Viscount Keith was Elphinstone, and recalled that he had given proof of his goodwill to an officer of that name who had been wounded and taken prisoner by the French at Waterloo. In his optimism he clutched at any straw and he built up hopes from this coincidence. But Lord Keith, as his letters to his wife testify, described the Emperor as a 'ragamuffin', and was not at all well disposed towards him at the time, although his attitude was to change as he made increasing contact with the Emperor. Keith in fact found his mission irksome. He was stiffer than usual, and adopted the tone of a high-ranking officer. He was cold and composed. Interviews became painful. As the scales fell from the Emperor's eyes, he became angry, and the tragic consequences of the decision he took at the Île d'Aix, albeit under pressure of circumstances, to surrender to the English now dawned on him. 'I decided to give myself up', he exclaimed, 'and I would not have done that to any other Allied power, for I would have been at the mercy of the whims and will of a monarch. In submitting to England I put myself at the mercy of a nation.' The position Napoleon adopted, confined as he was in English waters, may be gathered from his letter to the Prince Regent; and this position he was determined to defend against all and sundry, as the most solid basis for present and future protests. His letter to the Prince Regent would be the charter regulating his relations with England. He was convinced that his view was the correct one and justified by the occasion. It was however a view diametrically opposite to that of the British Cabinet.

The letter to the Prince Regent, then, repays close study. Did Napoleon really hope that on reading this petition, drawn up in his own hand though inspired by Savary, the Prince Regent was going to turn himself into an angel of mercy? The future George IV may have been a toper and a libertine, but he was a man of strong views, who had never wavered in his hostility to Napoleon. He was a cynic into the bargain. (In 1821, on learning of the death of 'his greatest enemy' he exclaimed 'My God, it's her', meaning Queen Caroline; but the news was of Napoleon's death.) Like a good constitutional monarch, he passed the letter on to the Cabinet—without comment.

Turning for the moment to the actual terms of the letter, it is to be noted that the Emperor (overlooking the joint Allied declaration of the previous March putting him outside the law) states that he comes 'like Themistocles' to throw himself on the hospitality of the British people—an implication recalling that Themistocles had sought the hospitality of his enemy Artaxerxes. This classical allusion was noted by the Prince Regent, although in point of fact there was little similarity between the case of the Athenian and Napoleon. Analogies are dangerous.

But overlooking this minor difference, we come to the essential part of the letter, which reads thus: 'I come to throw myself upon the hospitality of the British people. I put myself under the protection of their laws, which I claim from Your Royal Highness...'

There are three points here. 'I come' — that is, I, Napoleon, of my own accord as a free agent (so he supposes) — to 'throw myself on the hospitality of the British people'; that is, I ask for its hospitality, convinced that it will be extended in accordance with a generous tradition and I would be the victim of bad faith if it were otherwise. That is, without any warrant from anyone for so thinking, he takes the view of the situation most favourable to himself and has the brilliant idea of saying to the man who in spite of all, he hopes, will receive him: 'Here I am and I give myself up to you of my own volition. You are a worthy enemy and I have confidence in you.' He is putting himself on a higher plane than his enemy and inviting him to display the greatest magnanimity. It is a bold gesture, of a piece with Napoleon's baring his breast to the soldiers of the 7th Regiment and asking, 'Which of you would fire on his Emperor?'

There is also the legal, or purportedly legal, argument. 'I put myself under the protection of English law.' In truth, notwithstanding Montesquieu and Voltaire, notwithstanding La Valette and Caulaincourt, (poor advisers hastily consulted at Malmaison), notwithstanding Las Cases, who had learnt nothing from a long stay across the Channel, Napoleon had little idea of the exact scope of the laws he expected to protect him. It was sheer presumption on his part to seek their protection. Yet it was this protection to which he laid claim, to use his own strong expression, from the sovereign; as if the latter owed it to him, whereas it was not his to give.

We have got to the heart of the theory which Napoleon, in ignorance real or pretended, was maintaining relentlessly and with the obstinacy of despair on the poop of the *Bellerophon*, where he was a prisoner. And if the words *Habeas Corpus* were not actually used in the letter to the Prince Regent, they were obviously implied, as events were to prove.

Habeas Corpus — these two words have gone round the world and have acquired a meaning complete in themselves, although taken by themselves they convey no more than the two opening words of a Papal Bull. The words *Habeas Corpus* were originally the opening words of a series of ancient orders of the English courts, or 'writs', from the Latin 'breva'. They were drawn up in Latin, and of a procedural nature — summonses, warrants, writs. Thus there was the writ of *Habeas Corpus ad testificandum*[1] by which a judge compelled the attendance before the court of a person in custody to give evidence in person; the writ called *Habeas Corpus ad respondendum* compelling a person sentenced to imprisonment by a lower court to be brought before a higher court to answer a more serious charge; that of *Habeas Corpus ad deliberandum* for transferring a person from one place of detention to another to face trial. Application for the issue of these writs was made to the court or to a judge of a superior court who, having heard the applicant's case, and having found for him, gave to the writ the form of a peremptory order, '*Habeas Corpus*': that is, 'You, gaoler, will produce X in person etc....'

During the reign of the Plantagenet Edward I a lawyer invented a new kind of order, the writ of *Habeas Corpus ad subjiciendum* which was to make it possible to bring immediately before an open court, any person claiming that he had been wrongly arrested.

Over the centuries this writ came to be used in English procedure with the approval of successive parliaments, so that it became of prime importance in protecting the subject against arbitrary arrest. Already by Napoleon's time its machinery had been perfected. However, before describing it, even in outline, it is necessary to refer to its origins in the deepseated love of liberty that has existed since time immemorial in the English heart. Did not the rebel barons of the thirteenth century force King John at Runnymede to sign the Great Charter that has become famous as the *fons et origo* of British liberty, this Great Charter article 39 of which provides 'that no free man shall be arrested or imprisoned or deprived of his land, or outlawed, or exiled, or in any way prejudiced, nor will the Crown proceed against him save by the judgments of his peers'. This Great Charter was to be consolidated in succeeding centuries with additional provisions. Then came the Tudors. They were dictatorial. If Parliament gave way to them, the explanation was to be found in the struggle of the Crown with its too powerful subjects, the problems of the Reformation and the threat of the Armada. Their successors, the Stuarts, wished to continue and intensify this despotic policy, and came to regret it. People and Parliament rebelled, and from 1628 strengthened the

---

[1] Not to be confused with the writ of *sub poena ad testificandum* which, as we shall see later, McKenrot resorted to for the Emperor's benefit. (See Chapter VII.)

ancient orders and writs which protected the liberty of the subject. In 1640 both Houses passed the *Habeas Corpus Act*. In 1679 came the *Habeas Corpus Amendment Act* and in 1688 the *Bill of Rights* capped the edifice.

This legislation ensured that in future no person could be arrested, as was possible under the early Stuarts when the Court of Star Chamber could order anyone to be arrested *per speciale mandatum Domini Regis*. Now, anyone claiming to have been illegally arrested or detained on English soil had the right, either himself or by someone on his behalf, to apply to any Judge for an order requiring the person detaining him to bring him in person before the Court, which would determine whether his arrest was lawful. It was important to ascertain, not the merits of the case against him, but the legality of his arrest or detention. Was his detention arbitrary? Then there must be jurisdiction to determine it; the person under arrest must be released as soon as it is established that his detention is illegal. If it is illegal, the Judge has no option but to release him forthwith. We are face to face with a *festinum remedium*, an urgent order which gaolers, judges and all officers concerned must comply with, or suffer severe penalties. Thus it was difficult for an Englishman, or a foreigner in England, under normal circumstances to languish in prison. This was the result of the remarkable tenacity of the English people over the centuries who, preferring the reality to the form, had reaped their reward well before the beginning of the nineteenth century.

This general rule was however always subject to important limitations. The protection of *Habeas Corpus* was effective in peace time, but an Englishman, or foreigner on English territory, could not avail himself of it if the country were rent by civil war, or invaded, or in a state of rebellion. These guarantees were then automatically suspended (as they could not be if it were merely a question of conspiracy or riot) by operation of Common Law, acting on Cicero's principle *inter arma silent leges*: 'in time of war the laws are silent'. Then Government officials and officers of the Crown, taking priority, when the situation so requires, over the administration of justice, will have *carte blanche* to act as they think fit in the national interest. On the other hand, when peace and order are re-established, the courts, whose jurisdiction has been temporarily superseded, will be restored to their normal functions, which can be exercised retrospectively. Thus any

Île d'Aix, *La Maison de l'Empereur*

Île d'Aix, *La Chambre de l'Empereur*

Captain Sir Frederick Maitland R.N.

Napoleon's letter of surrender to the Prince Regent, official copy
(reproduced by gracious permission of Her Majesty the Queen)

Facsimile of original draft in Napoleon's own hand
(reproduced by courtesy of the present Baron Gourgaud)

Napoleon in 1815. Portrait by Pierre–Paul Prud'hon.
(reproduced by courtesy of the Prince de la Tour D'Auvergne)

Napoleon in the *Épervier*'s boat before embarking on H.M.S. *Bellerophon* in the Basque Roads (Aquatint by Jazet) An imaginary scene (see p. 43)

Admiral Lord Keith

Sightseers in Plymouth Harbour. H.M.S. *Bellerophon* in centre with Napoleon on board. (Oil painting by J. J. Chalon, 1816)

person aggrieved by these exceptional measures, or who has been the victim of arbitrary action during the suspension of Common Law and its protective remedies, will from then on have the right of recourse to the appropriate court whose duty it will be to decide if the acts complained of can be justified as a consequence of war, civil war, or rebellion. If they cannot be so justified, those who have been prejudiced by arbitrary or high-handed acts of the executive will obtain redress of their grievances and be awarded damages. If the acts were justified, the complaint will be dismissed. Either way there could be anxieties for state officials, since they may be compelled to defend themselves in an indefinite number of proceedings. For this reason, English law has for a long time allowed the Executive, so as to protect itself against a multiplicity of actions, to ask the House of Commons to pass an Act of Indemnity, which has the effect of absolving the members of the Government and officials from any liability where they have acted in good faith and in the public interest. This absolute power is the prerogative of Parliament. It alone can modify, by Statute, the Common Law, which, in the absence of a written constitution, includes constitutional law. And even when, there being no actual state of war or rebellion, Common Law does not allow sufficient powers to the Government in a given situation, Parliament, if it thinks fit, will strengthen them, for example, by conferring additional powers of arrest where that is desirable.

Furthermore, at Common Law, if the Crown in time of peace has no power to detain anyone without due cause, it has this power in wartime, and even if the war is being conducted in a foreign theatre, the paramount prerogative to imprison, without reason given, any enemy national within its territory. As to British subjects and neutrals, special rules apply, varying with the circumstances.

That being the law in Napoleon's time, it is not difficult to conclude, as did the English lawyers, that the Emperor could not have recourse to *Habeas Corpus*. England and Napoleon were at all material times at war, even if, for his part, Napoleon desired peace. He was an enemy alien on British soil, even if he had surrendered in the hopes of special treatment. According to the view which gained widest acceptance, he was a prisoner of war, and if there was any doubt about that, Parliament would silence any argument by resorting to an Act of Indemnity. Such a measure would be, in effect, as regards all persons concerned, the best way of sealing the Emperor's fate. And this even if the measure were unnecessary, for Lord Eldon, whilst advocating the passing of an Act of Indemnity, took the view that it would be enough for the British Government to refrain from terminating the state of war between England and Napoleon to justify detaining him indefinitely.

It may be that the British Government was influenced by political considerations in reaching its decision. But that is beside the point. In such a contingency it intended to have the law on its side. If Napoleon invoked the law of England in the sincere belief that the Government would help him, he was mistaken. On the other hand, if he were doubtful of the effectiveness of English law, and had, after being cornered at the Île d'Aix, brushed aside all considerations in surrendering to the English, then one must admire his good psychology in surrendering and the ability he displayed, in view of his desperate case, by appealing to the Prince Regent.

This tedious but necessary explanation out of the way, we will trace in the pages which follow the moving and unequal fight of the prisoner Napoleon against a detention he at all times regarded as arbitrary, and against the assault on his person of which, in his view, the British Cabinet was guilty.

CHAPTER 5

The Emperor is Told

I like historians to be either simple or first-rate. The simple ones, who bring nothing of themselves to their work save the care and diligence to collect everything that comes to their notice and to record everything in good faith, do leave our judgment free for perceiving the truth.

MONTAIGNE

THE INITIAL PROTESTS of Napoleon had, it is hardly necessary to say, no effect on the policy of the British Government. The implementation of its decision took its course.

The island of St Helena was finally decided upon as the place of internment. Napoleon was to be transported there in a faster vessel than the *Bellerophon*; this was the *Northumberland,* her sails soon to be in sight. Maitland was instructed to break the news unofficially on 30 July, so as to lessen the shock of the official notification arranged for the next day. At 10 a.m. on 31 July, Lord Keith repaired on board *Bellerophon* accompanied by Lord Bathurst's representative, Major-General Sir Henry Bunbury, Under-Secretary of State for War and the Colonies, the bearer of the British Government's decision—a man of grave appearance, honourable and loyal and not without insight, as his description of the Imperial prisoner bears out.

At Napoleon's request Lord Keith attempted to translate orally the British Government's note. This task being beyond him, he passed it to Sir Henry Bunbury, who had a better command of French. The note read as follows:

Admiralty, 28th July, 1815.

My Lord,

As it may be convenient to General Buonaparte that he should be apprised without further delay of the intentions of the British Government respecting him, your lordship is at liberty to communicate to him the information contained in this letter.

It would be inconsistent with our duty to this country and to his Majesty's allies if we were to leave to General Buonaparte the means or opportunity of again disturbing the peace of Europe and renewing all the calamities of war. It is therefore unavoidable that he should be restrained in his personal liberty to whatever extent may be necessary to secure our first and paramount object.

The island of St Helena has been selected for his future residence. The climate is healthy, and the local situation will admit of his being treated with more indulgence than would be compatible with an adequate security elsewhere. Of the persons who have been brought to England with General Buonaparte, he will be allowed to select (with the exception of Generals Savary and Lallemand) three officers, who, together with his surgeon, will be permitted to accompany him to St Helena. Twelve domestics, including the servants of the officers, will also be allowed. It must be distinctly understood that all those individuals will be liable to restraint during their attendance upon him and their residence at St Helena: and they will not be permitted to withdraw from thence without the sanction of Government.

Rear-Admiral Sir George Cockburn, who is appointed to the chief command at the Cape of Good Hope and the adjoining seas, will convey General Buonaparte and his attendants to St Helena, and will receive detailed instructions respecting the execution of that service. Sir George Cockburn will probably be ready to embark in the course of a few days, and it is therefore desirable that General Buonaparte should make without delay the selection of the persons who are to accompany him. I have the honour to be, etc.

MELVILLE.

The record of this memorable interview, during which so terrible a decision was conveyed to the fallen Emperor, is in the British archives, in the form of reports made at the time by Lord Keith and Sir Henry Bunbury to their respective superiors, Lord Bathurst, Secretary of State for War and the Colonies, and Lord Melville, First Lord of the Admiralty. They bear the stamp of truth and are most moving.

We went on board the *Bellerophon* between eleven and twelve o'clock. Buonaparte was alone in the inner cabin. We were announced and were admitted immediately. After I had been introduced and Buonaparte had put a few trivial questions, Lord Keith produced a copy of the letter from Lord Melville containing the orders of his Majesty's Government, and tendered it to Buonaparte. He inquired if it was in French; and on being told that it was in English, he observed that it would be useless to him, and that it would be necessary to translate it. Upon this Lord Keith began to read it aloud in French, but Buonaparte appeared not to hear distinctly, or not to comprehend: and after a line or two had been read, he took the paper from Lord Keith's hands and proposed to me that I should translate. I believe he meant that I should make a written translation, but I preferred reading it aloud in French.

Napoleon listened attentively to the whole without interrupting me, and appeared as if he had previously been aware of what was to be communicated to him. At the conclusion, Lord Keith asked Buonaparte if he wished to have a written translation made; but he answered no, that he comprehended the substance perfectly, that the translation had been sufficiently good. He received the paper and laid it upon the table, and after a pause he began by declaring his solemn protest against this proceeding of the British Government; that they had not the right to dispose of him in that manner; and he appealed to the British people and to the laws of the country. Buonaparte asked what was the tribunal, or if there was not a tribunal, where he might prefer his appeal against the illegality and injustice of the decision taken by the British Government. 'I am come here voluntarily', he said: *'me placer sur les foyers de votre nation* and to obtain the rights of hospitality. I am not even a prisoner of war. If I were a prisoner of war you would be bound to treat me *selon le droit des gens*; but I am come to this country a passenger on board one of your ships of war, after a previous negotiation with its commander. If he had told me I was to be a prisoner, I should not have come. I asked him if he was willing to receive me and my suite on board and to carry me to England. Captain Maitland answered that he would — and this after having received, and after telling me that he had received the special orders of his Government concerning me. *C'était donc un piège qu'on m'a tendu.* In coming on board a British ship of war, I confided myself to the hospitality of the British nation as much as if I had entered one of their towns — *un vaisseau, un village, tout cela est égal. Quant a l'île de Sainte-Hélène, c'est l'arrêt de ma mort.* I protest against being sent thither, and I protest against being imprisoned in a fortress in this country. I demand to be received as an English citizen. I know indeed that I cannot be admitted to the rights of an Englishman at first. Some years are requisite to entitle one to be domiciled. Well, let the Prince Regent place me during that time under any surveillance he may think proper. Let me be put in a country house in the centre of the island, thirty leagues from the sea. Place a commissioner about me to examine my correspondence and to report my actions; and if the Prince Regent should require my parole, perhaps I would give it. There I might have a certain degree of personal liberty, and could enjoy the liberty of literature. In St Helena I should not live three months: with my habits and constitution it would be immediate death. I am used to ride twenty leagues a day. What am I to do on this little rock at the end of the world? The climate is too hot for me. No, I will not go to St Helena: Botany Bay is better than St Helena. If your Government wishes to put me to death, they may kill me here. It is not worth while to send me to St Helena. I prefer death to St Helena; and what good is my death to do you? I can do you no harm. I am no longer a sovereign. I am a simple individual. Besides time and affairs are altered. What danger could result from my living as a private person in the heart of England under surveillance, and restricted in any way the Government might imagine necessary?'

Buonaparte returned frequently to the circumstances under which he had come on board *Bellerophon*, insisted that he had been perfectly free in his choice, and that he had preferred confiding to the hospitality and generosity of the British people, rather than take any other course. 'Why should I not have gone to my father in-law or to the Emperor Alexander, who is my personal friend? We have become enemies because he wanted to annex Poland to his dominions—and my policy prevented him; but otherwise he was my friend, and he would not have treated me in this manner. If your Government acts thus, it will disgrace itself in the eyes of Europe; and even your own people will disapprove and blame its conduct. Besides you do not know perhaps what a feeling my death will create both in France and Italy, and how greatly the character of England will suffer if my blood rests here. There is a high opinion of the justice and honour of England. If you kill me, your reputation will be lost in France and Italy, and it will cost the loss of many Englishmen. There never has been a similar instance in the history of the world; and what was there to force me to the step I took? The tricolour flag was still flying in Bordeaux, at Nantes, at Rochefort. The army had not by then surrendered. I could have joined them; or if I had chosen to remain in France, what could have prevented my remaining concealed for years among a people who were all attached to me? But I preferred to settle as a private individual in England.'

Buonaparte reverted again to his negotiations with Captain Maitland, the assurance that he should be carried to England, the honours and attentions shown to him by Captain Maitland and Admiral Hotham. 'And after all, this has been a snare laid for me. If you now kill me, it will be an eternal disgrace to the Prince Regent, to your Government and to the nation. *Ce sera lâcheté sans exemple. J'ai offert au Prince Régent la plus belle page de son histoire.* I am his enemy and I throw myself on his mercy. I have been the greatest enemy to your country. I have made war upon you for twenty years and I do you the highest honour, and give you the greatest proof of my confidence, by placing myself voluntarily in the hands of my most inveterate enemies. Remember what I have been, and how I stood among the sovereigns of Europe. One courted my protection, another gave me his daughter; all sought my friendship. I was an Emperor, acknowledged so by all the Powers of Europe except Great Britain, and she had acknowledged me and treated me as First Consul of France.'

Then, turning to the table and laying his fingers on the paper, 'And', said he, 'your Government have not the right to style me General Buonaparte. I am at least as much of a sovereign in Elba, as when I was on the throne of France. I was as much a sovereign in Elba, as the king was in France. We had each our flags. I had my flag,' he repeated. 'We had each our ships, our troops. To be sure,' he said smiling, 'mine were on a small scale. I had six hundred soldiers and he had two hundred thousand, *mais enfin je lui ai fait la guerre; je l'ai battu, je l'ai chassé du pays, et je l'ai détrôné*. But there was nothing in all this to alter my rank or to deprive me of my position as one of the sovereigns of Europe.'

Napoleon spoke with little or no interruption from Lord Keith or myself. He sometimes paused as for a reply. I could only say that I was little more than bearer of the despatches to Lord Keith; that I was not authorized to enter into discussions; and that I could only undertake to hear General Bounaparte's representations, and to communicate them to the King's Ministers. I observed that I felt convinced that the chief motive which had made the Government fix upon St Helena was that its local situation admitted of his enjoying there a greater degree of indulgence than could be allowed in any part of Great Britain. Buonaparte immediately said '*Non, non pour Sainte-Hélène, je n'irai pas; vous ne voudriez pas y aller vous, Monsieur, ni vous, my lord*'. He then renewed his protest against being imprisoned or sent to St Helena. '*Je ne sors pas d'ici, je n'irai pas à Sainte-Hélène. Je ne suis pas un Hercule, mais vous ne m'y mènerez pas! Je préfère la mort ici!* You found me free, send me back again. Replace me in the state you found me, and which I quitted only under the impression that your Admiral was to land me in England. If your Government will not do this, and will not permit me to reside here, let me go to the United States. But I appeal to your laws, and I throw myself on their protection to prevent my being sent to St Helena, or being shut up in a fortress.'

Buonaparte inquired when the *Northumberland* was likely to arrive and to be ready to sail, and he pressed the Admiral to take no step towards removing him from the *Bellerophon* until the Government should have been informed of what had passed on this occasion, and should have signified their final decision. He added that, as to going on board the *Northumberland,* he could not do it, '*Je n'irai point. Je ne sortirai pas d'ici.*'

Lord Keith appeared to think that even if the *Northumberland* should arrive, this delay might be granted. As he addressed me, I answered that I could give no opinion upon this point, and that it rested with his lordship to decide. Buonaparte urged me to aquaint His Majesty's Government without the least delay of what had passed. I told him that I should despatch a written report immediately; and that I should remain myself at Plymouth until the next day, in case he should have anything further to state. Lord Keith asked if he would wish to put his answer in writing. He said, '*Non, ce Monsieur entend bien le français. Il fera le procès-verbal. Il est dans une situation éminente et il doit être honnête homme ; il rendra au gouvernement la réponse que j'ai donnée.*'

After some pause, Buonaparte began again. He went over the same ground, dwelling particularly on his having been free to come or not, and his having decided to come here, from understanding that Captain Maitland, acting according to the orders of his Government, would undertake to bring him in safety; upon the illegality of sentencing him to death or imprisonment; and his desire to appeal formally to the laws and people of England; upon the disgrace which would attach to the nation, and particularly to the Government. He repeated his desire to live in England as a private citizen under any restrictions, and with a commissioner to watch him, 'who would be also of great use to me for the first year or two, in showing me what I ought to do' and he added, 'I will give my word of honour that I will not hold any correspondence with France, and that I will not engage in any political affairs whatever'. Finally, he repeated his fixed determination not to go to St Helena.

We made our bows and retired. In a few minutes Buonaparte sent for Lord Keith again. I did not return with his lordship, who remained a very short time.

H. E. BUNBURY.

We now reproduce Lord Keith's report to Lord Melville, the First Lord of the Admiralty. The Admiral knew the contents of the report submitted by Sir Henry Bunbury to the Minister of War. He associated himself with it in the following terms:

Ville de Paris in Hamoaze
31st July, 1815.

My Lord,

Accompanied by Major General Sir Henry Bunbury I this morning went on board His Majesty's ship *Bellerophon,* for the purpose of communicating to General Buonaparte the intentions of His Majesty's Government as pointed out in Your Lordship's letter of the 28th instant.

After common civilities had passed, I began to read to General Buonaparte the first paragraph of my instructions; the remainder were successively explained by Sir Henry Bunbury.

General Buonaparte in reply adverted to the state of his health and expressed his doubts whether he could be compelled to quit England, repeating his wish for permission to live here as an individual. He also observed that he had no power, that he could do no harm, that he would give his word of honour to hold no communication with France, that he could have remained there with the Army, that it was not an act of necessity but of choice which induced him to throw himself into the hands of the English; and that he now claimed that protection out of justice and humanity.

These arguments were urged in various points of view, and very frequently repeated and he also put the question individually both to Sir Henry Bunbury and myself (a question to which we, of course, made no reply), what we should do under the circumstances, adding himself, 'Go to St Helena? No—No. I prefer death. I am determined not to go on board the *Northumberland.*'

Although he repeatedly solicited our good offices, he declined writing any observations on the paper I left him explaining the intentions of His Majesty's Government, adding at the same time that he felt he was speaking to 'men of honour' to which I replied that it was my duty to report precisely what he wished to be conveyed to my superiors. I repeatedly proposed to retire, the General to the last to urge the same style of argument. A conversation that passed at a second interview when Sir Henry Bunbury was not present, Your Lordships will find detailed in the enclosed. I have the honour to be, etc.

KEITH
Admiral

Upon re-entering the cabin [writes Lord Keith] he asked me to advise him. I replied, 'I am an officer and have discharged my duty. I have left the heads of my instructions with you, in order that you may observe upon them if you consider it necessary'. I added, 'Sir, if you have anything more to urge, I must beg to call in Sir Henry

Bunbury; to which he replied, 'Oh, no, it is unnecessary'. He then said, 'Can you, after what has passed, detain me until you hear from London?' To which I answered 'That will depend upon the arrival of the other Admiral, of whose instructions I am ignorant'. He then said, 'Is there any tribunal to which I can apply?' I replied, 'I am no lawyer; but I believe none. I am satisfied there is every disposition on the part of the British Government to render your situation as comfortable as is consistent with prudence'. He immediately took up the papers from the table and said, with animation, 'How so St Helena?' to which I observed, 'Sir, surely it is preferable to being confined in a smaller place in England, or sent to France, or perhaps Russia'. '*Russie? Dieu m'en garde!*' was his reply. I then withdrew.

The same evening Napoleon sent Lord Keith a final letter in which he repeated and confirmed the protests he had made that morning and which were included in Sir Henry Bunbury's report. The Emperor added:

> I am certain that Your Lordship and the Under-Secretary of State will give a faithful account of all the points I made in proof of my rights. I have placed, and still place, my confidence in the honour of the Prince Regent and the protection of your country's laws.'

NAPOLEON
On board the Bellerophon.

At the same time as he sent in his official report, Sir Henry Bunbury made pencil notes on a pad, for later use in his *Memoirs*, which were a painting from life of the Emperor:

'Napoleon's height appeared to me to be about five feet six inches, and he is stockily built. His neck is short, and the head appears the larger for it; his face is square, especially towards the jaw, and he has a pronounced double chin. He is bald about the temples and the hair on the upper part of his head is very thin, but long and ragged, looking as if it were seldom brushed. In his movements Napoleon lacks grace, but in the course of the interview he made few gestures. The carriage of his head is very dignified. He is somewhat obese, and this is more apparent because his uniform, open at the neck, is only buttoned as far as the belt: from this point its skirts part to left and right, leaving revealed most of his white waistcoat.

'This uniform is green, with red facings, plain but finished off by gilded epaulettes and buttons. Buonaparte carried at his side a small old-fashioned sword with an incised hilt. He wore the broad ribbon of the Legion of Honour, and the silver eagle worked on his breast. I also noticed three small decorations attached to one of his button-holes. His hat, which he kept for the most part under his arm, was fairly large, unadorned except for a tiny tricolor cockade at the side.

In the course of the interview Napoleon dipped repeatedly into his snuff-box, which was oblong, very simple, and with I believe four miniatures or medallions on the lid.

Napoleon's eyes are grey, the pupils large, his eyebrows thin, his hair brown, his complexion pallid, his flesh rather puffy. His nose is well shaped, the lower lip short, a good mouth, but teeth bad and dirty; he shows them very little. His expression was serious and almost melancholy, and showed no sign of anger or strong emotion.'

As for Napoleon's companions, Sir Henry Bunbury drew the following thumb-nail sketches: of Bertrand, he said, 'his manners gentlemanlike, his countenance grave and thoughtful'; of Savary, 'a handsome man, but something sinister in the working of his countenance, his manners restless, and betokening the fears which were excited by the knowledge that he was one of those proscribed by Louis XVIII'; of Lallemand, 'likewise under proscription, a thick set man, coarse in his appearance, and sullenly determined in his looks'; of Montholon, 'rather insignificant'; of Las Cases, 'not far removed from being a little old quiz; nervous and fidgety'; of Gourgaud, 'a youngish man, with a smart genteel air and some-what of a coxcomb'.

Having decided upon the deportation order, the British Cabinet lost no time in securing the agreement of the Allies, who on 2 August unanimously associated themselves with it, and with understandable despatch, declaring:

1. That Napoleon Buonaparte is the prisoner of the Allies.

2. That the custody of Napoleon is delegated to the British Government which will select a place of detention and will be in control of security arrangements.

3. That the Allied Powers, Russia, Austria and Prussia will send Commissioners to the place of detention, and they may be joined by a French Commissioner.

Having reached this agreement, the British Government could now dispose of the prisoner. The *Northumberland* was in dry dock, but would be undocked with all despatch.

CHAPTER 6

The Defender

Before I be convict by course of law,
To threaten me with death is most unlawful.

SHAKESPEARE

IF THE British Government acted with vigour, if the Admiralty
pressed on with arming the *Northumberland* (which, being recently
returned from a foreign station, needed a refit), and if it overbore
the dissatisfaction of members of her ship's company who thought
they were entitled to a spell on shore, the reason was to be found in
the attitude of a section of liberal opinion which gave cause for
anxiety. This party came out in favour of Napoleon, the man
condemned. It thought that he had been treated too harshly,
considering that he had thrown himself on the generosity of the
English people and on the protection of their laws. That was the
view of the Duke of Sussex (younger brother of the Prince Regent),
Lord Holland and his wife (both faithful supporters of Napoleon),
of Brougham (the M.P. one day to become Lord Chancellor), his
colleague Hobhouse, and many others. They favoured the policy of
conciliation associated with Fox,[1] and, lest it be thought that they
were animated by disingenuousness and sentimentality, they
genuinely wanted to bring a conflict that had raged so many years
to an humane and generous conclusion.

Napoleon, quick to see his opportunity, thought to profit from
this movement in his favour. It was not too late, he decided, to
fight a final battle, into which he would throw himself with all the
obstinacy born of despair, just as he had committed the Old Guard
in the closing stages of Waterloo. He and his friends would try to
make contact with a few persons holding liberal views, whilst his

[1] Henry Richard Vassall Fox, 3rd Baron Holland, nephew of Charles James
Fox, whose political lead he followed. His succeeding to the barony at an early
age debarred him from sitting in the Commons. He was in France at the out-
break of the Revolution and he was sympathetic to its early developments. His
wife, a famous Whig hostess, held a political salon at Holland House for many
years. Lord and Lady Holland were, both in 1815 and during his captivity in
St Helena, tireless in their efforts on Napoleon's behalf.

76

supporters found a spokesman in the eminent barrister Capell Lofft,[1] who had published the following spirited letter in the Whig *Morning Chronicle* of 31 July:

Sprotton Hall, 30 July, 1815.

To the Editor of *The Morning Chronicle.*

Sir,

The intelligence that the great Napoleon will not be permitted to land, and is to be sent perhaps to St Helena, is almost overwhelming to me, though long accustomed to suffer much, and to expect everything.

I know not that the Emperor can be regarded as a prisoner of war. From a view of all the circumstances that affect his person, and situation, and of his coming hither, I am of opinion that he cannot.

But if he could, it is not, nor has been for two centuries, the custom of Britain thus to treat her prisoners.

Could we try him? — I know not by what right either we, or any, or all of the Confederates could.

Can we without trial take his life? — This were far worse than to kill a prisoner recently taken in battle.

Can we then exercise such a power over the personal and inherent dignity and honour, far dearer than life, of such a Personage, and to send him to lonely imprisonment in a deserted far distant island?

Buonaparte with the concurrence of the Admiralty is within the limits of British local allegiance. He is temporarily considered as a private, though not a natural born subject, and as such within the limits of 31 Car. II, the *Habeas Corpus* Act our 2nd Magna Charta, that no subject, being an inhabitant or resident of England etc. shall be sent prisoner into Scotland, or to places beyond the seas (c. 12). All persons within the Realm of England, which includes the adjoining seas, are temporary subjects if aliens, or permanent if natural born.

Though not on the British soil he is within the protection of British law. If at Plymouth, he is in a British county. An *Habeas*

[1] Capell Lofft (1751–1824), son of Christopher Lofft, secretary to Sarah, Duchess of Marlborough, and of Anne, sister of Edward Capell, publisher of one of the best editions of Shakespeare. He was a member of the English Bar and an extreme Whig. A convinced opponent of slavery, he devoted no mean talents to the service of justice and humanity. He incurred the censure of a court for having tried to save a young servant girl who had been sentenced to death for a trifling theft. Corresponded with Fox, Wilberforce, Hazlitt and others. He was long one of the friends of Napoleon 'who could always count on his support'. After 1815 he travelled in Europe, and died in Italy, at Moncalieri.

Corpus if issued, must be obeyed: and no doubt would be willingly obeyed by the Captain of the *Bellerophon*. It would be issuable, being Vacation, by the Chancellor, the Chief Justice of England, or other of the Judges at their house or chambers, immediately, founded on an affidavit. And if all communication with the *Bellerophon* is shut out, which might enable Napoleon himself to make the application, the imprisonment of any individual within the limits of the English laws and constitution concerns the dignity, the liberty and the rights of every Englishman; and constitutes fault or error in respect to this all protective law, which being remedial must be most liberally construed

I am of opinion that deportation, or transportation, or relegation, cannot legally exist in this country, except where the law expressly provides it on trial and sentence.

It cannot be expected that many authorities should be quoted in such a peculiar case: neither is it necessary, as it differs from the common cases of every day, chiefly in the greatness of the Person who is its object.

Divested of these circumstances it is this. He voluntarily came on board; Captain Maitland received him, agreeably, as the Captain understands, to secret orders. If he is debarred of all communications, and correspondence, and forbidden to land, this must be by some order, and for some purpose. And the Writ of *Habeas Corpus* is the legal mode of investigating, as to all persons, whether their liberty be legally or illegally restrained, and all restraint of liberty is illegal, of which the legality is not clearly and strictly proved.

I know of no law of ours which supports such a conduct, as is asserted to have already taken place, and to be further determined. And I trust we are not yet come to this, that the will and practice of the Confederates is a law to us.

We think with horror of the power assumed by the Pope over the persons, consciences, liberties, lives, dominions and entire nations of those who were not his subjects. I know not in what the power assumed by the Confederate Powers is more tolerable.

I am, yours sincerely,
CAPEL LOFFT.

It will be seen that Capell Lofft's arguments were a direct attack on the Government's position. His plausible advocacy, promoted by a paper as influential as the *Morning Chronicle,* could not fail to give the Cabinet cause for anxiety. Moreover, when the paper published its correspondent's letter, it commented editorially that it had received more than a hundred letters from all parts of

England, and that Bonaparte's situation had excited very great interest. The paper did not doubt that the administration would introduce an Indemnity Bill to regularize its position (and also to authorize His Majesty to detain Bonaparte for as long as he thought fit) since the action it had taken was illegal.

While Capell Lofft was conducting his campaign, Napoleon and his faithful staff were busy seeking ways of avoiding the cruel fate that threatened them. They had succeeded in bribing sailors who were good swimmers to make contact with the shore carrying their messages in zinc tubes.

A curious document has been discovered entitled *Thoughts on Napoleon Buonaparte and his civil and political position on landing in England.* It is set out under three headings:

(a) Is Napoleon a prisoner of war?
(b) What are the British Government's rights if Napoleon is a prisoner of war?
(c) Finally, in view of Captain Maitland's instructions to receive him and his suite and to take them to England, had Napoleon not placed himself under the protection of the laws of this country?

It goes on to stress that Napoleon could, as he pointed out to Major-General Sir Henry Bunbury, have rejoined his armies, re-grouped south of the Loire under Davout, Bordeaux being held by General Clauzel and Nantes by General Lamarque.

Moreover the author of the note seems to have had a two-fold object, for not only did he urge the solution of the legal problems raised, but he wished to influence public opinion. In the margin of this document there were words to this effect: 'Compile a list of quotations for the newspapers and let this document be the basis for a case at once powerful and worthy of the ability and high-mindedness of a good Englishman who is also worthy of the gratitude and help of all great and generous hearts'.

Who was the author of this note? To whom was it addressed? No one knows. But it is probable that its author was Savary, and that it was addressed to an eminent English jurist, and influential liberal, Sir Samuel Romilly.[1] It was to him that Savary, fearing for

[1] Sir Samuel Romilly (1757–1818). As his surname indicates, he was of French extraction. His ancestors were Huguenots who settled in London after the revocation of the Edict of Nantes. A famous advocate, he was celebrated for his legal knowledge and integrity of character.

his life should he be extradited, had already sent a request for a consultation, which follows. Savary got in touch with Sir Samuel Romilly through another, and very persistent, liberal, Sir Francis Burdett, who had been recommended to him by a certain Lady Clavering, whose acquaintance the émigré Las Cases had made when she was a young French milliner, and who had since made her way in Society.

The following are the principal passages in Savary's letter:

> *H.M.S. Bellerophon,*
> *off Plymouth,*
> *1st August, 1815.*

Sir,

The reputation you enjoy as well as the integrity of your character have emboldened me to seek the benefit of your experience in a situation in which the honour of the British flag is as much compromised as my personal safety has been in trusting it. I will explain my position and ask for your advice.

My name suffices to explain how I was brought to this country in the wake of the greatest misfortune history records.

I threw in my lot with the Emperor Napoleon when a combination of circumstances compelled him to seek asylum on board one of your nation's warships, having previously received assurances that his person would be inviolate and that he would have the protection of English law which takes priority over the decision of Ministers.

It was with such feelings of confidence that we embarked on board *Bellerophon,* whose captain assured us that he had authority to receive us: consequently we considered ourselves to be under the protection of English law.

Since our arrival at this port we have, ostensibly, on account of the law or custom relating to aliens, been subject to confinement strict to the point of being ridiculous, which even the most scrupulous courtesies have not made tolerable.

Yesterday an official arrived to notify the Emperor of the Cabinet's decision to order him to St Helena. [Then Savary envisaged the possibility that the English authorities would refuse to let him go with Napoleon and keep him prisoner in England. He took exception to such a course. But there was a worse possibility: that the English, having no more interest in him, would simply return him to France, where proscription lists that could endanger his life had just come out.]

Sir, I ask your support and beg of you to put my claim before the proper authority. I have informed the Commanding Officer of

H.M.S. *Bellerophon* that I will not leave his ship save to seek the protection of a magistrate, before whom I bring my case. If force is used against me I will use force in return.

Having made that clear, Sir, I ask you to advise me as to the probable consequences, if I have the misfortune to kill someone in the course of defending myself, before I am given an assurance that my personal safety will be safeguarded.

This is my situation. I ask your aid in improving it.

Yours, etc.,
THE DUKE OF ROVIGO.

In his *Memoirs* Sir Samuel Romilly relates that on receiving this appeal he decided to call on Lord Eldon. Lord Eldon was reassuring, but he added 'Please say no more about it'. Whereupon Romilly, whilst respecting the Lord Chancellor's confidence, replied to Savary that he was active on his behalf. As to Savary's urge to resist, Romilly brushed it aside: 'Do not use force. Should you kill anyone you will be judged a murderer. You will be tried and sent to the gallows.' Sir Samuel, though he did not see to what court Napoleon could have recourse, had certain reservations. He thought it strange that the measures taken in regard to Napoleon were decided upon before Ministers knew for certain what had transpired between Maitland and Bonaparte and how the latter had reacted to his reception on board a British warship. But this question, though open, was shelved for the time.[1]

Savary, on behalf of Lallemand and himself, sent appeals to Lord Keith and to the First Lord of the Admiralty, Lord Melville, but the two Frenchmen were unaware that they had the formidable support at this juncture of Captain Maitland. The latter, as it happened, by-passed the usual channels, probably because it was for him no longer a question of correct procedure but of honour, and he wrote direct to the First Lord of the Admiralty as follows:

H.M.S. Bellerophon
Plymouth Sound
31st July, 1815.

My Lord,
    I am induced to address your Lordship in consequence of having observed, in the intimation delivered to Napoleon Buonaparte of the

[1] In view of the facts the opinion of Sir Samuel Romilly was not altogether sound, for the *Bellerophon* reached England on the 24 July and it was not until 31 July that the Government informed Napoleon of its decision to exile him to St Helena. In the interim the Cabinet had deliberated on a number of occasions.

number of persons allowed to accompany him to the Island of St Helena, that the names of Savary and Lallemand are expressly excepted, which, together with their being proscribed in the French newspaper, has created in them a belief that it is the intention of His Majesty's Government to deliver them up to the King of France. Far be it from me to assume such an idea; but I hope your Lordship will make allowances for the feelings of an officer who has nothing so dear to him as his honour, and who could not bear that a stain should be affixed to a name he has ever endeavoured to bear unblemished. These two men, Savary and Lallemand (what their characters or conduct in their own country may be I know not) threw themselves under the protection of the British flag; that protection was granted them with the sanction of my name. It is true, no conditions were stipulated for, but I acted in the full confidence that their lives would be held sacred, or they should never have put foot in the ship I command, without being made acquainted that it was for the purpose of delivering them over to the laws of their country. I again beg leave to repeat to your Lordship, that I am far from supposing it to be the intention of His Majesty's Government to deliver these men over to the laws of their country; but, as they are strongly impressed with that belief and I look upon myself as the cause of their being in their present situation, I most earnestly beg your Lordship's influence may be exerted that two men may not be brought to the scaffold who claimed and obtained at my hands the protection of the British flag.

I have the honour to be, etc.,

F. L. MAITLAND.

This letter is a vital piece of evidence. It surely justifies the inference that if Maitland had made any precise promises in regard to the Emperor, he would certainly have taken care to recall them.

In the event, Savary and Lallemand were not deported to France, but were nevertheless held prisoner by the British and taken to Malta. Released after seven months Lallemand went to America and Savary to Smyrna, where on 14 July, 1816, a year to the day after he first embarked in *Bellerophon*, he addressed to Sir Samuel Romilly, to whom he thought he owed his safety, a letter of thanks, and at the same time, in compliance with a request of the Emperor, a memorandum on the circumstances of the latter's surrender. On joining *Northumberland* the Emperor had urged Savary to draw up such a memorandum, which would include an account of the false promise made by Captain Maitland. The following are the material passages in the documents:

Dear Sir,

It is only now that I am once more at liberty, that I am able to thank you for the answer you were kind enough to make to the letter I had the honour to send you just over a year ago, when I thought myself to be in danger on board *Bellerophon* in Plymouth harbour. Everything that has happened since convinces me that it was due to your generous interest that I was not sent back to France, as the Government of that country so strongly urged. During my long imprisonment I resolved that I would offer you my heartiest thanks.

After having hinted in a roundabout manner that Sir Samuel Romilly might help him to bring proceedings in defamation against those who had alleged that he was responsible for the death of Captain Wright, Savary goes on as follows:

You will recollect that I was one of the men who followed the unlucky fortunes of the Emperor, and by Government order, was sent to Malta and held a prisoner there in conditions of the greatest secrecy for seven months; where I was joined by seven other officers in similar case. We sought in vain for reasons to justify this extraordinary measure. The real reason for our severe treatment was the fear that I, or my companions, might reveal everything that happened both before and after the Emperor's arrival on board *Bellerophon*. Why they should have been afraid of our revelations I do not know, but whatever their reasons, I felt myself bound by the promise I had made to the Emperor at our farewell meeting: that I would lay before you all the details relating to this part of his story.

He knew both your name and the character you bore: it was enough to command his trust, and it is with the same respect with which I used to receive his orders at the height of his fortunes that I now carry out the last wishes he expressed in their decline. I have no desire for this chronicle of events to cause trouble, but if the use you choose to put it to involves attaching my name to it, then, Sir, I am a man of honour, and no matter what dangers may result, I beg you to treat the matter without thought for me; even if it should cost me my life, I would be proud to think that it was you who had placed me in that position.

Savary's account is entitled *Notes on the events between the Emperor's escape from Elba and his voyage to St Helena*, and runs to seventeen closely written quarto pages. It will suffice here to quote a passage dealing with Savary's talks with Maitland before the Emperor embarked in *Bellerophon*:

Asked about the safe conducts, Maitland said that he thought it unlikely the Government would allow the Emperor to leave for the United States. 'Then', said Savary and Las Cases, 'where do they suggest he goes?' Captain Maitland replied, 'I have no idea (although I am practically certain that the Government will not allow him to go to the United States). What objection would there be to his going to England? That might solve all his difficulties.'

M. de Las Cases said that he had no authority to discuss that question, but that personally he thought the Emperor had not considered it, perhaps because he was afraid that relationships might be strained because of the deep-seated misunderstanding between himself and the British Government. Moreover, he enjoyed a mild climate, and pleasant conversation; in America he hoped to find both, without having to fear any ill treatment.

Maitland replied that it was a mistaken idea that the English climate was cold and damp, and that in several counties, notably Kent, it was as mild as many places in France, and that the enjoyments of social life were infinitely greater than anything he would meet with in America. As for ill feelings that he might expect from the English, all of this would be dissipated by coming to live amongst them under the protection of their laws; that he would be completely safe and out of his enemies' reach; even the Ministry itself would be unable to harass him. 'With us there is no arbitrary government, it is conducted in accordance with our laws. I believe', he went on, 'that the Government would adopt the same measures to ensure both his tranquillity and that of the country, as it did in the case of his brother Lucien.'[1]

M. de Las Cases again made it clear to Captain Maitland that it was not for him to discuss these matters, but that he had followed the conversation attentively and would report it to the Emperor, and he put the question, 'If the Emperor decided to go to England — and I would lend him my best efforts to persuade him — could he and his suite make the journey aboard your ship?' Captain Maitland's answer was that he had no orders about it, but that he would refer the matter to his superior officer, and that if the Emperor asked for a passage before he received an answer, he would in any case, undertake to receive him on board.

This conversation was immediately reported to Napoleon, who on 14 July sent Lallemand and Las Cases to Maitland to parley as though under a flag of truce. The interview of the previous evening was resumed and at its conclusion Las Cases caused a message to be

[1] Captured at sea on his return to the United States in 1812, and interned at Thorngrove in Worcestershire.

sent to the Emperor informing him that 'If he decided to go to England, Captain Maitland was ready to receive him on board and put his ship at his disposal.'

That is Savary's version. The reader will be the judge of its importance. Savary wanted Sir Samuel Romilly to publish it in the English press, but he refused. Moreover, the document was unsigned.

It has been worth quoting Savary's memorandum here, since it relates to the vital talks that preceded Napoleon's surrender. Without wishing to draw any conclusion, it seems rather odd that a British naval officer would expatiate at length on the climate of Kent, the English county nearest to France, and the one least likely to be selected for accommodating such a prisoner.

CHAPTER 7

Napoleon's Desperate Situation

Bold of your worthiness, we single you
As our best-moving fair solicitor.

SHAKESPEARE

THE SUM OF the activities of English liberals had not altered the situation where the Emperor was concerned. Every argument, and every step taken, foundered against the unshakeable determination of the British Government to take the drastic step of banishing Napoleon.

The throne of Louis XVIII was insecure, and England, driving force of the Coalition though she was, depended on it. What would have happened if the Allies, instead of supporting it, had jibbed at the St Helena solution and had refused to allow Great Britain to act as the Emperor's guardian, insisting instead on joint guardianship of the Allies? Or even on a trial, in which the British judges would have been in the minority? To what pressures and subterfuges would England and Europe have had to resort? Moreover, at the back of the British mind lay dormant the Common Law principle that an enemy alien, whilst he may be kept prisoner, may not be summarily executed. This idea informed the acts of the Cabinet, which wished to preserve Napoleon's life. In such circumstances, it was important to adhere firmly to the course decided on, and remove Napoleon from Plymouth without delay.

The position of Napoleon, his passage on the *Northumberland* decided, was thus desperate, when an unexpected last-minute legal manœuvre was executed on his behalf, which, had it been successful, would have altered the course of events. The hand of Capell Lofft perhaps may be seen in all this. As he had once said, 'The Emperor can count on me'.

The proper procedure for removing a person alleged to be unlawfully detained on board ship in English waters, was to take out a writ of *Habeas Corpus ad subjiciendum,* calling on those detaining him to produce his body before a competent judge with a view to his release. This procedure was not followed in Napoleon's case.

What chance would there have been that the writ would be granted, since in the Government's contention, Napoleon was a prisoner of war, and so outside the scope of the writ? But was there not, in the whole armoury of legal weapons, one which would achieve a similar result by compelling the Government to delay the departure for St Helena and so enable the Emperor to gain time? Strange as it may seem, such a weapon was found.

At the beginning of 1815, one McKenrot, or MacKenroth, had been sued for defamation in the King's Bench Division by Admiral Sir Alexander Cochrane,[1] commanding the West Indies Squadron. McKenrot was of German extraction, born in London, where he studied law. He was of a sullen disposition, excitable, and had a stormy career. Eventually he obtained a minor judicial appointment in Tortola, an island in the Lesser Antilles. He saw to it that he did not have a quiet life there. He had hardly arrived before, wishing to draw attention to himself, he picked a quarrel with Admiral Cochrane, whom he accused of incompetence, even cowardice, for not attacking a French squadron weaker than his own. This squadron was commanded by Admiral Willaumez, accompanied by Jérôme Bonaparte, and cruising in the same waters. Sir Alexander Cochrane, not prepared to have his character blackened by such a nonentity, brought an action in London against McKenrot. McKenrot, in preparing his defence, did not hesitate to ask leave of the King's Bench to call as witnesses to character, not only Admiral Willaumez and Jérôme Bonaparte, but the Emperor himself. He clearly wished to create a stir and impress the public. This seems more likely when it was obvious that he was already showing signs of excessive excitability (he was to end his days in Bedlam). However, leave to call the witness was easily obtainable, the issue of the writ being automatic on payment of the prescribed fee. The Registrar of the Court was not concerned with the quality of the witnesses nor with their places of residence.

[1] Sir Alexander Cochrane (1758–1832) younger son of the 8th Earl of Dundonald, had a distinguished naval career and took part in several naval actions before the Peace of Amiens. He then came back to England and was elected to Parliament. In 1806 in H.M.S. *Northumberland* he distinguished himself at the Battle of San Domingo (as second in command). It was in those parts that he became, in about 1814, a victim of McKenrot's ill-will. Commander-in-Chief, Plymouth, 1821. Died in Paris in 1832 and buried in Père Lachaise.

It is probable that this quaint procedure would have remained a dead letter. Was it likely that the three persons named would appear before an English court—if the course of events had not been deflected by destiny? There was Waterloo, where, as Chateaubriand put it, 'the world was at the mercy of a gambler's throw', there were the sad stages on the journey to the Atlantic coast; the Emperor leaves France, reaches English territorial waters and *ipso facto* finds himself within the jurisdiction of the English courts.

It is in these circumstances that the absurd document which McKenrot had obtained in June from the King's Bench (the writ whereby Napoleon Bonaparte was summoned to come and give evidence in *Cochrane versus McKenrot*) whilst he was in France and out of reach, suddenly acquired a great importance. For Napoleon, being now in English territorial waters, in the event of his being served with the writ, would have to comply with the requirements of English law and appear as a witness before the King's Bench. The whole process was to his advantage, as his departure for St Helena could be delayed until the conclusion of the action. The unforeseen opportunity it provided was grasped by a zealous intriguer on Bonaparte's side, and the writ became a powerful weapon in a legal wrangle of considerable importance to the Emperor.

The record of this writ is still in the office of the King's Bench and runs as follows:

> George the Third, by the grace of God, of the United Kingdom of Great Britain and Ireland, King, Defender of the Faith, to Napoleon Buonaparte, Admiral Willaumez, and Jérôme Bonaparte, greeting: We command you and every one of you that all other things set aside and ceasing every excuse, that you and every one of you be and appear in your proper persons before our right trusty and well beloved Edward Lord Ellenborough, Chief Justice assigned to that Plea in our court before us on Friday the tenth day of November by nine of the clock in the forenoon of the same day, to testify to the truth according to your knowledge in a certain action in our court before us, in our said Court depending between Sir Alexander Forrester Cochrane, Knight, Plaintiff, and Antony MacKenrot, Defendant, of a Plea of Trespass on the part of the defendant, and at the aforesaid day by a jury of the country between the parties aforesaid to the Plea aforesaid to be tried; and

that you nor any of you shall in no wise omit under the penalty of one hundred pounds.

Witness: Edward Lord Ellenborough, in Westminster, this fourteenth day of June, in the fifty-fifth year of our reign.

One does not have to be learned in the law to realize that this writ has nothing in common with any of the orders of *Habeas Corpus*. Its issue is a matter of judicial routine, and is known as *subpoena* (abbreviation of *sub poena ad testificandum*) its normal effect being to bring a witness before the court on two conditions: first that the person named is within its jurisdiction, i.e., upon British territory, and the other that he be at liberty. If he is lawfully in custody the *subpoena* will be null and void and it will then be necessary to have recourse to a *Habeas Corpus ad testificandum* which, incidentally, will not prevent him giving his evidence while under guard.

What was Napoleon's position? He was clearly upon English ground in territorial waters, and thus satisfied the first condition. As to the second, opinions differ, the liberals (like Capell Lofft, who apparently behind the scenes advised McKenrot to resort to this procedural juggling) bitterly disputed the legality of the detention of the Emperor. In the *Morning Chronicle* Capell Lofft had developed this argument, and if one agreed with it, it followed that Napoleon was only a *de facto* and not a *de jure* prisoner of war, and therefore in a position to be served with the writ; in which event his guardian Admiral Keith, commanding the Channel and Atlantic squadrons, to which the *Bellerophon* belonged, would, under pain of severe penalties, be obliged to comply with the Order of the Court of King's Bench, one of His Majesty's ships not being able to detain unlawfully a witness duly summoned by one of H.M. Judges.

Such a contention, although it had no chance of carrying the day, since the Government would not be deterred by any objections, and was determined to send Napoleon to St Helena at the earliest moment, nevertheless created an awkward dilemma for the Government which suited the book of Napoleon's friends. For if the Royal Navy, by declining to comply with a writ served on a Napoleon under illegal restraint, had the audacity not to put Napoleon ashore, it laid itself open to the charge of flouting the law. This would foster a movement in Napoleon's favour. On the other hand, if the naval authorities complied with the writ it would indicate that they were uncertain as to the legality of their prisoner's detention, and he, once ashore, would have the advantage of several months' respite pending the hearing of *McKenrot versus Cochrane,* fixed for 10 November—a most unwelcome prospect for the Government. It is obvious that a man who was both astute and courageous would perceive great advantage in such a complicated situation. However, even if it is conceded that, since the two foregoing conditions were satisfied, the summons was valid, it was still necessary to serve it on the person named therein, in accordance with the English rules of procedure; that is, on the proper person through a process server, or by the party himself, in this case McKenrot. It must be delivered to Napoleon personally or, failing him, his guardian, Lord Keith himself. That is why McKenrot, who was undoubtedly in collusion with Capell Lofft and who knew that the sailing of the *Northumberland* was imminent, resolved to travel post-haste to Plymouth in an attempt to serve the process despite the obstacles which would be put in his way. He would not leave the execution of such a delicate matter to anyone else.

At the same time as these lawyers' devices were afoot, Lord Keith wrote to the First Lord of the Admiralty:

> You cannot imagine what a crowd we have here. The inns are full and the sea covered with swarms of small boats. I conceive that I must be particularly vigilant, for the 'General' (Napoleon) and his suite are convinced that once they set foot on shore, no power on earth can bring them back again. They are determined to disembark. It is all they talk of and they are becoming very aggressive.

On the 2 August, Lord Melville replied to Lord Keith:

> You will receive what is perhaps, and most probably, unnecessary—I mean an official instruction ON NO ACCOUNT to permit Buonaparte to come on shore. In some of the newspapers a notion is held out that he may be brought out of the ship by a writ of *Habeas Corpus.* The serious public inconvenience and danger which would arise from such an occurrence, even though he may not escape and be remanded by the judge as a prisoner-of-war, renders it indispensably our duty to prevent it, and also to protect you, or rather Captain Maitland and Sir George Cockburn, by the peremptory order which we have sent you.

The next day, the 3 August, McKenrot left for Plymouth, arriving there on the morning of the 4th. But he was already too late: he had been forestalled, as we have seen, by the Admiralty's instructions. On receipt of Lord Melville's message Lord Keith acted with remarkable speed and skill.

As soon as McKenrot got to Plymouth, he made for the dockyard and saw the Superintendent, Sir John Duckworth, and asked permission to serve the writ on Napoleon. Duckworth replied that it was not a matter for him; the Emperor was Lord Keith's prisoner. McKenrot hastened to Lord Keith's house. He found only his private secretary, James Meek. He saw Lady Keith, and questioned her. No one knew where the Admiral was. He was said to be in the Sound, on board one of the ships of his squadron, but no one knew which. Meek, appreciating the importance and danger of McKenrot's proceedings, and of McKenrot's blandishments, hastily despatched a note to Lord Keith on board the flagship, the *Tonnant,* informing him of the disturbing appearance of McKenrot. The latter hurried to the harbour. He saw, at no great distance the *Bellerophon* hove-to and awaiting the slightest wind to leave, in accordance with Lord Keith's orders, a berth too close to the shore. He made for this ship (he wrote later of having the inexpressible delight of seeing the Emperor and one of his generals at the window of the Admiral's cabin). McKenrot, waving the writ, indicated that he wished to come alongside, but one of the ship's boats patrolling near the *Bellerophon* ordered him to keep off. As McKenrot persisted, the officer of the watch threatened to shoot. Hailed by McKenrot, this same officer in an unguarded moment replied that the Admiral was on board the *Tonnant*. McKenrot rowed hard towards that ship, which he approached on the port side. Keith was in fact on board, but as McKenrot was approaching, he left the ship by the starboard side and made off in a pinnace that was too fast for McKenrot's boat. Out-manœuvred, McKenrot returned to the shore, and wrote the following letter, which he left at Lord Keith's residence together with a copy of the writ.

> *King's Arms Tavern,*
> *Plymouth Dock,*
> *Aug. 4, 3 o'clock p.m.*

My Lord,

I arrived this morning from London with a writ issued by the Court of King's Bench to subpoena Napoleon Buonaparte as a witness in a trial impending in that Court.

I was extremely anxious of waiting on your Lordship most

humbly to solicit your permission to serve such process on your said prisoner: but unfortunately could not obtain any admittance into your presence, neither at your own house nor on board H.M.S. *Tonnant,* where your lordship was said to be.

I humbly entreat your lordship to consider that an evasion to give due facility to the execution of my process would amount to a high contempt against that honourable Court from whence it issues, and that under the continuance of such circumstances, I shall be under the painful necessity of making my return accordingly.

Leaving the issue to your Lordship's discretion, I shall remain here until tomorrow night; but to remove all doubts from your mind, I beg to enclose a copy of the writ for your perusal...

Having completed this, the indefatigable detective returned to the harbour, and made once more for the *Tonnant,* which Keith had just joined after a cruise, and which, thanks to a rising wind, was slowly making for the open sea at the same time as the *Bellerophon.* But as McKenrot was approaching, the Admiral, run to earth, transferred from the *Tonnant* to another ship, the *Eurotas.* McKenrot, spurring on his oarsmen, directed them towards this vessel; meantime the Admiral bolted for Cawsand Bay where he lay hid for some hours. Later, having shaken off McKenrot, he returned to his barge, and rowed to the nearest ship, the *Prometheus,* which as an added precaution he only left after night-fall to return to the *Tonnant.*

When Lord Keith took delivery of McKenrot's letter on the 5 August the *Tonnant* and the *Bellerophon* were out of reach. On the same date Lord Keith wrote to his wife—that he was at sea waiting for Sir George Cockburn and *Northumberland.* It was fortunate he had left his house before the process-server arrived. The man had followed him, and if he had caught him up, Keith would have been dragged before the Court, and then he would have been Boney's keeper until November. On the same day, Lord Keith wrote to his niece, Miss Elphinstone, that the crowds had obliged him to make off and wait for the arrival of Sir George Cockburn. He had had a writ of *Habeas Corpus* brandished at him. But he was now on the high seas.

Notwithstanding these misadventures, McKenrot would not admit defeat. His unremitting efforts enabled him to get a letter through to the Emperor in which he kept him posted on his actions. He aimed at providing Napoleon with a quiet place of residence in England until November, when the Courts would be sitting again and the Cochrane case would be called. But as these plans had come to nothing and Napoleon was about to be sent off to St Helena without any further legal ado, McKenrot, ever resourceful, told the Emperor that he meant to request the Court of King's Bench to bring him back in November. The authorities in the island, he declared, would have to obey this injunction.[1] In the meantime, went on McKenrot, Parliament would make a strong protest against this violation of the Constitution — both the harsh restraint practised upon Napoleon, and his illegal deportation.

Further, on his return to London, McKenrot sent a long report by messenger to the Empress Marie-Louise. He besought her to lose no time in writing to the Prince Regent of England begging his good offices for the release of her illustrious husband. He asked the Empress for an immediate reply and even suggested he should come in person to Vienna to receive her orders.

So far from answering these pathetic appeals, Marie-Louise was content to pass the document on to Metternich, who on 29 September, 1815, gave it to his English colleague, Lord Castlereagh, Secretary of State for Foreign Affairs. All he did was to cause a senior official at the Foreign Office, Joseph Planta, to make a true copy which, duly certified, is now in the British archives.

One realizes the difficulty the British Government would have found itself in had McKenrot's scheme succeeded. It was certainly a strange one, the product of a distorted mind, and presents difficulties to anyone who tries to write about it, yet at the same time it was inspired by loyalty. In fact, it was not a question of an absurd voyage undertaken by a crank, but of a legal procedure which, if it had been effective, would have helped Napoleon.

Sir Walter Scott, in his *Life of Napoleon*, thus sums up the affair:

> Some newspaper, which was not possessed of a legal adviser to keep it right in form, had suggested (a tenderness, we suppose, to public curiosity) that the person of Napoleon Buonaparte should be removed to shore by agency of a writ of *Habeas Corpus*. This

[1] He said so, but it was not certain; since the island of St Helena was the property of the East India Company it might have been held to be outside British jurisdiction. Furthermore, Napoleon was now the prisoner, not of England alone, but of all the Allies.

magical rescript of the Old Bailey, as Smollett terms it, loses its influence over an alien and prisoner of war and therefore such an absurd proposal was not acted upon. But an individual, prosecuted for a libel upon a naval officer, conceived the idea of citing Napoleon as an evidence in a court of justice, to prove, as he pretended, the State of the French navy, which was necessary for his defence ... Although this was a mere absurdity, and only worthy of the laughter with which the anecdote was generally received, yet it might have given rise to inconvenience, by suggesting to Napoleon, that he was, by some process or other, entitled to redress by the Common Law.

CHAPTER 8

The Governor's Orders

There's a guid time coming.
WALTER SCOTT

EVEN BEFORE McKenrot's arrival at Plymouth, the Secretary for War and the Colonies had dispatched to Rear-Admiral Sir George Cockburn, commanding the squadron being assembled for passage to St Helena, precise instructions on the attitude to be adopted towards Napoleon as from the date of sailing from England. These instructions, it seems to us, should be quoted *in extenso*.

When General Buonaparte shall remove from the *Bellerophon* to the *Northumberland* it will be a fit moment for Admiral Sir George Cockburn to direct an Examination of the Effects which the General shall have brought with him.

Admiral Sir George Cockburn will allow all Articles of Furniture, Books, and Wine which the General may have brought with him to be transhipped on board the *Northumberland*.

Under the Head of Furniture is to be included his Plate, provided it be not to such an amount as to bespeak it to be rather an article of convertible property than of domestic use.

His Money, Diamonds, and Negotiable Bills of every description are to be given up. The Admiral will explain to the General that it is by no means the intention of the British Government to confiscate His Property, but simply to take the Administration of these Effects into their own Hands for the purpose of preventing their being converted by him into an Instrument of Escape.

The Examination must be made in the presence of some person appointed by General Buonaparte, and an Inventory of the Effects so to be retained must be signed by this Person as well as by the Rear Admiral or anyone appointed by Him to make out the Inventory.

The Interest on the Principal (according to the amount of the Property) will be applicable to his Maintenance, and the disposition of it, in that respect, left chiefly to his own choice.

He will, for that purpose, from time to time, communicate his wishes to the Admiral until the new Governor of St Helena arrives, and to the Governor afterwards; and unless the proposition be objectionable, the Admiral or Governor, as the case may be, will give the necessary orders, and the Bills will be paid by Bills drawn upon His Majesty's Treasury.

In the Event of his Death the disposition of his Property will be determined by his Will, the Contents of which he must be assured will be strictly attended to.

As an Attempt may be made to represent part of the Property as belonging to Persons in his Suite, it must be understood that the Property of those who go out with him, is subject to the same regulations.

The disposition of the military allotted to guard him must be left to the Governor, the Governor being instructed to attend to the wishes of the Admiral in the instances hereafter to be mentioned.

The General must be always attended by an Officer appointed by the Admiral or Governor as the case may be—if the General be permitted to move beyond the Boundaries where the Sentries are placed, the Officer should be attended by one orderly at least. In the Event of Ships arriving—so long as they continue in sight the General must be confined within the Boundary where the Sentries shall be placed. He must during that Interval be prohibited from all Intercourse and Communication with the Inhabitants. They who accompany him to St Helena must be subject at this period to the same regulations—They are to reside with him, and it is to be left to the discretion of the Admiral in the first instance, and to the new Governor afterwards, to establish such regulations with respect to them at other times as may appear expedient.

The Admiral will not take on board any Individual belonging to General Buonaparte's Suite for the purpose of conveying him to St Helena with the General, except with his full consent, after it has been explained to him that he thereby becomes liable to all the Regulations which it may be deemed necessary to subject him for the security of the General's Person.

The General must be given to understand that in the Event of his attempting to escape, he will afterwards be subject to close Custody, and they who go out with him must also understand that if they shall be detected in contriving means for his Escape they will be separated from him and placed in close custody.

All letters addressed to him or his Attendants, must first be delivered to the Admiral, or to the Governor as the case may be, who will read them before they are delivered to the Persons to whom they are addressed. All Letters written by the General or his Attendants must be subject to the same Regulation.

No Letter, which has not been transmitted to St Helena by the Secretary of State, should be delivered to the General, or to those who accompany him, if it be written by any Person not resident in the Island, and all their Letters addressed to Persons not resident in the Island must be sent under cover to the Secretary of State.

The General must be given clearly to understand that the Governor and Admiral are strictly instructed to forward to His Majesty's Government any Wish or Representation which they may think proper to make to the British Government: and in that particular, they are not at liberty to exercise any discretion ... but the paper on which such applications or representations may be written must be left open for their joint inspection, in order that in transmitting it, they may be enabled to accompany it with such observations as they may think expedient.

Until the arrival of the New Governor, the Admiral must be considered entirely responsible for the Security of General Buonaparte's Person, and His Majesty's Government entertains no doubt of the disposition of the actual Governor to concert with the Admiral for this purpose.

The Admiral is authorized to keep the General on board or re-embark him, if the Security of his Person cannot, in the Admiral's opinion, be otherwise obtained.

On the Representation of the Admiral on his arrival at St Helena, the Governor will take measures immediately to convey either to England or to the Cape, or to the East Indies, according to the circumstances of the case, such non-commissioned Officers and Privates in the military Corps at St Helena as the Admiral may deem expedient to release from their Military Duty on the Island, by reason of being Foreigners, or on account of their general Character and Disposition.

If there are any Foreigners in the Island, whose residence there appears to the Admiral calculated to be instrumental to General Buonaparte's Escape, measures must be taken for their removal.

The whole Coast of the Island and the Vessels and Boats frequenting it must be placed under the control of the Admiral. He will regulate the places which Boats may frequent, and on his representation the Governor will station a sufficient guard at those places at which the Admiral may think precaution necessary.

The Admiral will take the most effectual Steps to watch the arrival and departure of every Ship so as to prevent any Intercourse with the Shore, except such as he may approve.

An order for preventing, after due notice, foreign Ships and Ships belonging to the private Trade, from resorting to St Helena will be forthwith given.

7

If the General should be attacked by any serious indisposition,
the Governor and the Admiral will each direct a Medical Person,
in whom they may have confidence, to be in attendance on the
General in addition to his own Medical Assistance, and direct
them severally to report daily on the state of his health.

In the Event of his Death, the Admiral will give orders for his
Body being conveyed to England.

WAR DEPARTMENT 30 July 1815.

The contents of this document which, thanks to Captain Maitland's efforts, had percolated to Napoleon and his companions,
left them in a state of amazement and indignation. They had just
been sent away from Plymouth. They were on the high seas. The
slight links they imagined they had with the English shore were
severed. Napoleon sent Lord Keith a written protest which he was
to repeat and enlarge upon the next day. The Emperor retired to
his cabin, and did not appear for some time.

A dark pall covers the ship and its despairing passengers. At the
prospect of leaving for St Helena, Marshal Bertrand's Irish wife
tried to throw herself overboard through one of the windows in the
poop. The Emperor, who had contemplated suicide a year before
at Fontainebleau, thought once again of ending his life. Those
about him were even willing to kill him and each other, like that
former member of the Convention, Romme[1] and his friends, who
stabbed one another in 1795, to avoid the guillotine. A boat
prowled about the *Bellerophon* during the night. Maitland was
anxious and doubled the sentries. This feverish atmosphere could
not last. Madame Bertrand became calmer, the suspect boat
turned out to be imaginary. The faithful band decided, in all the
circumstances, against extreme measures. Napoleon, consoled by
Las Cases, came to terms with life.

[1] Charles Gilbert Romme (1750–1795). Distinguished mathematician.
Deputy for Puy-de-Dôme, during the Convention. Reformed the calendar.
Accused of complicity in the revolt of the Mountain on 1st Prairial in Year III,
and condemned to death along with his friends.

CHAPTER 9

Napoleon leaves the *Bellerophon*

*After all I am a great believer in everyone fulfilling
his destiny. May mine be fulfilled.*

NAPOLEON

AFTER SEVERAL DAYS of complete confusion, the passengers in the
Bellerophon, now tacking under the lee of Berry Head, descried
the great silhouette of *Northumberland* approaching. Lord Keith
thought that these waters would be the most convenient for the
trans-shipment of the Emperor and his companions.

On 6 August Lord Keith and Sir George Cockburn were on
board the *Tonnant* engaged on the painful task of working out the
best way to deal with the last formalities before the final departure.

Towards the end of the afternoon the two admirals met Count
Bertrand, who asked for an interview. Bertrand gave the names of
those who were to make up the Emperor's retinue. Lord Keith
insisted on a written list, which Bertrand undertook to provide.
Bertrand further requested that Las Cases be included in the
capacity of private secretary to fill the vacancy caused by a certain
Dr Maingault, who had joined the *Bellerophon* at Rochefort, but
who jibbed at the prospect of going to St Helena. This request
was favourably received. It was then necessary to appoint a
surgeon for the Emperor. Dr O'Meara, the surgeon of the
Bellerophon, was willing to go. He spoke Italian, a language the
Emperor had not forgotten. Planat de la Faye was to be left out.
That was probably unfortunate: he had qualities that would
have been useful to the Emperor. The servants presented no
problem, except for the Pole, Piontowski, who had been in Elba,
and for that reason was not acceptable to the Admiral. The
baggage was to be examined on the next day, 7 August.

On the evening of the 6th, Lord Keith, accompanied by Sir
George Cockburn, and attended by his secretary, Charles Meek
(whose presence as a witness was thought to be useful after Sir
George Cockburn had left) went on board *Bellerophon* to be
received by the Emperor. With great persistence, Napoleon

adverted to the same grievances and repeated his case. Once again, and with reason, he was offended at being addressed as 'General'. 'But', he added, 'that is a mere trifle compared with the violation by your Government of every principle of justice, humanity and generosity as regards myself. Such a violation will not be approved by the English nation nor by Europe'. The two admirals replied that they could not discuss the matter.

Sir George Cockburn then asked the Emperor at what time he would be ready next day to leave *Bellerophon*. Napoleon answered that he would do so at a time convenient to the Admiral, preferably after breakfast, which he usually took at about ten o'clock.

The next day, the 7th, Las Cases handed Lord Keith the following letter, signed by the Emperor:

My Lord,

On leaving Plymouth, I sent you my protestations regarding the conduct observed with respect to me. Yesterday, when you did me the honour of coming to see me with Admiral Cockburn, I repeated that protestation.

It appears to me, however, that without knowing the effect of these complaints, you require that I should leave the *Bellerophon* to go on board a vessel destined to conduct me to the place of my banishment. I sent you the Count de Las Cases, to beg you to give up to him, first, the signed act of the Authority which, without previous enquiry, without having heard the captain of the *Bellerophon*, or any of those who received me, has arbitrarily decided that I am a prisoner of war, contrary to the most patent facts; since it is notorious that I came of my own free will and in good faith, as is proved by my letter to the Prince Regent, of which the captain had taken cognisance before receiving me.

I beg you, my lord, to give up to him, secondly, the signed decision which, after having declared that I was a prisoner, ordered that in contradiction to the laws of the country and those of hospitality, I should be dragged from the *Bellerophon*, to be deposited at a distance of two thousand leagues on a rock lost amid the ocean, in the middle of tropical heats. It is evidently a sentence of death which it would be difficult to resist in a temperature so broiling, and which is so sudden a change.

My lord, I claim, — I claim, I repeat, — the benefits of your laws, especially those of the *Habeas Corpus* Act. Once placed under your flag, in your harbour, with the tender of service and the promise of your captain, I cannot be arrested, deprived of any liberty, and placed in confinement, except according to your laws and by their forms.

Finally, I shall also beg you, my lord, to furnish me with, thirdly, the signed warrant of those, who, without any grounds except their own private resolution, wish to deprive me of my property, which is moreover of little value, and to impose on me persons as members of my suite, arrangements revolting to every person of delicate sentiments, and striking with surprise those who are acquainted with and who respect the laws.

The purport of these documents is necessary to me in judicially claiming the protection of your laws against them, as well as for making a solemn appeal to sovereign and people on this strange and singular affair.

You have yourself several times, my lord, expressed to me the pain which the execution of your orders has caused you. I therefore do not know that I need reckon on a better interpreter in enabling me to set forth the precipitation, the rigour, and the injustice with which I have been treated.

NAPOLEON

on board the Bellerophon, August 7th, 1815.

Lord Keith replied forthwith:

Sir,

I have received by the Count Las Cases the letter which you have done me the honour to address to me, and I beg to assure you that I lost no time in forwarding to my Government the protest you refer to. The order for your removal from the *Bellerophon* is imperative, and as an officer I am bound to obey it, but it is a document that must remain in my possession, in common with all other orders.

I have Captain Maitland's letters before me, by which it appears that nothing like a promise, or what could be construed into a promise, was made on his part; but on the contrary, a simple offer of good treatment and of being carried to England, and I am happy in thinking that both these objects have been fulfilled with all possible kindness and attention.

The orders respecting your property are addressed to Rear-Admiral Sir George Cockburn, and as they appear reasonable, and are only calculated to prevent an improper use of an excessive sum, I am sure they will be executed with all possible delicacy.

Of the laws I am not able to judge—my habits are of a different nature—but my study has always been to obey them in all the different countries I have visited. It is true that I have said, in the interviews that I have had the honour to hold with you, that it was a painful duty to communicate anything of a disagreeable nature to anyone — and I hope you will do me the justice to believe it true, but still I am to perform the duties of my situation.

I have the honour to be, etc.

KEITH
Admiral

The inventory of the belongings of the Emperor and his staff was to be drawn up on the 7th at 9.30 a.m. They included small articles of furniture, gold and silver plate, objects of value, souvenirs, books and pictures which Marchand had had the foresight to carry off on leaving the Elysée and Malmaison, and loaded for Rochefort to provide for emergencies. The British officials were tolerant in carrying out their unpleasant duty. Further, they were willing to turn a blind eye to members of the Emperor's retinue putting currency surplus to their shares in their belts, thus giving them a rather corpulent appearance. The diamond *rivière,* which Queen Hortense wished to give to the Emperor when they parted forever at Malmaison, was similarly disguised. A number of cases which had been left behind at Rochefort in the hurry of departure should have been included in the inventories. They were never recovered, neither were two light carriages, which Napoleon later regretted losing.

The checking of the inventory was completed at 11 a.m. Sir George Cockburn reported this forthwith to Lord Keith, who then sent his report to the Admiralty with all despatch. This report recorded the preceding events. We give a literal account of the last part, which relates with typically military brevity and exactness Napoleon's last moments on board the *Bellerophon,* which the Emperor regarded as his last bastion of English law. What modern chronicle is so evocative? In a few lines of official English the old sea-dog who had sailed the seven seas permits himself to reveal through his weather-worn exterior a streak of human warmth and sympathy which does him credit.

I then went on board the *Bellerophon,* but found that the General was engaged with Count Bertrand. It was some time before I saw him, when he repeated his former protestations, and added, 'I do not voluntarily go from this ship or from England. It is you, Admiral, who take me'. To this I replied, 'I hope, Sir, that you will not reduce an officer like me to use force towards your person'. He answered 'Oh no: you shall order me.' I replied, 'I shall attend you, at your convenience, in my barge. I beg not to hurry you'. He thanked me, and said he wanted to speak to Bertrand, whose wife I believe had no wish to go to St Helena. I then retired, and sent that officer into the after cabin.

It was nearly two hours after this period before the General finished his letters, conversation, and giving audience to those of his officers who were not going with him, some of whom shed tears, while he appeared to bear it well. He then came out of the cabin and said, 'I am at your orders'.

Before leaving *Bellerophon*, he thanked both Captain Maitland and his officers, for their kindness and attention while he was on board, adding 'My thanks also to the men'. Then he bowed to the whole company. Honours such as are paid to generals were rendered to him on the quarter deck. Then he went aboard my barge. He was followed by those men he had chosen to go with him, Count Bertrand and the Count de Montholon, with their wives, General Gourgaud and the Count Las Cases. I brought up the rear. Buonaparte, observant as ever, said to me, 'I see you are giving yourself the trouble of accompanying me. I thank you, Admiral'. In the barge the General appeared in the utmost good humour, recalling memories of Egypt, speaking of St Helena, of my name of Elphinstone, and many other things, now and then darting a glance at the ladies who were feeling sea-sick.

Arriving aboard *Northumberland*, Buonaparte was received by Sir George Cockburn at the break of the poop, and honours were rendered to him.[1] I accompanied him as far as his quarters, with which he seemed satisfied. He said, 'These are quite suitable, and,

---

[1] The surgeon of the *Northumberland*, William Warden, in one of his letters to his family which he later collected and published, has noted: 'From eleven o'clock until noon, we waited for Napoleon. Lord Keith, with great tact, had made it known that he did not in the circumstances wish to be paid the compliments due to an admiral, and Napoleon was only to be paid those due to a general, since England had never recognized him as Emperor. Accordingly, a detachment commanded by a captain was drawn up on the quarter deck, with orders to doff their hats, to be followed by three rolls of the drums, the officers then doffing their hats.'

However, the 1808 regulations ran: 'For generals and admirals honours should be rendered by a detachment commanded by a captain, while all officers salute and the drums beat a march.' If Napoleon was received with three rolls of the drums instead of a march, the regulation would not have been wholly complied with; three rolls being prescribed for a vice-admiral or lieutenant-general, and a march for an admiral or general. However, it is possible that Surgeon Warden, who was unlikely to have been an expert in military etiquette, was in error.

as you see, I have not parted from my little camp bed'. It was already installed.

While the flag ship *Northumberland* was awaiting the ships who were to sail in company with her, her officers received from the Prince Regent through the Secretary for War and Colonies, Lord Bathurst, and from the Admiralty, special instructions, the gist of which was:

> The Prince Regent, in resting such an important charge as the keeping of Buonaparte upon the officers of *Northumberland* desires that they be associated with him in his strong wish not to impose unnecessary restrictions upon Buonaparte's freedom of movement, always bearing in mind that their duty is to maintain a strict guard upon his person.
>
> Every attention, compatible with this duty, should be paid him, it being understood that the zeal, energy and devotion to duty of Rear-Admiral Sir George Cockburn will not allow any unwise reduction of vigilance.

It remains to mention an incident which created a stir at the time, but which must be seen in proportion. Montholon in his *Memoires* has conjured up, according to Octave Aubry, a moving scene in which, after the officers of his staff had given up their swords, the Emperor himself would have been asked to give his up. Lord Keith is reported to have said, in a voice overcome by emotion, 'England demands your sword'. 'The Emperor', goes on Montholon, 'with convulsive movement, put his hand on his sword. The old Admiral was dumbfounded; his tall figure seemed to become smaller, and his head, white after many years of service, fell forward on his breast ... the Emperor kept his sword.'

All this is pure fantasy on Montholon's part. Apart from the fact that it is unlikely that Napoleon wore his sword when he moved from one ship to the other, Lord Keith makes no mention of such an incident in his report, which suggests that it did not take place, or that it made little impression. Savary writes, however, that it was at the suggestion of Count Bertrand, although Las Cases claims the credit for this intervention, that Lord Keith did not require the Emperor to give up his sword—although Sir George, taking a stricter view, would have had him do so. But Lord Keith easily overcame Cockburn's scruples by remarking that 'as one returned his sword to an officer captured on the battlefield, all the more should one do so in General Buonaparte's case.'

CHAPTER 10

The Last Protest

FROM THEN ON the Emperor's fate was sealed. Of course, the decision to surrender was his, but even bearing in mind the pressure of events and that it was Savary's suggestion to write to the Prince Regent, Las Cases must be seen as the governing influence. He had been the chief go-between during the preliminary negotiations; he had relied on his doubtful experience of England; he had without due consideration deduced from some chance words of Maitland that if his (Las Cases's) master was unsuccessful in obtaining passports for the United States, he would obtain asylum in England and the protection of the law. Of the extent and nature of that protection neither Maitland nor Las Cases was aware, one of them being a sailor without legal training, and the other a Frenchman who, despite a long stay in England, had only gained a sketchy knowledge of her law.

That Maitland, pestered by Las Cases, in the interval between two glasses of brandy (which came from nearby Cognac and which the Captain's sense of hospitality compelled him to offer to his visitor) gave a general answer on the political and physical state of England, proud of its Common Law and healthy climate, there is no reason to doubt. But equally there is no reason to doubt that Las Cases, who was apt to confuse wishful thinking with facts, had attached a more positive meaning to Maitland's words than was justified in the circumstances, and did not take sufficient account of the reservations Maitland had expressed, which stemmed from his position as a serving officer, limited by his instructions and with no political standing. At the same time it is possible to imagine that the negotiations, conducted probably turn and turn about in two languages—for while Las Cases knew English well, Maitland knew some French—may have given rise to a certain amount of obscurity, and hence to misunderstanding.

However that may be, the turn of events, which had given evidence of his ineptitude and lack of judgement and flair, had deeply disturbed Las Cases. He was greatly distressed that Napoleon had been misled by his over optimistic reports. Deeply disappointed and embittered by the sight of his master in captivity, it was not surprising that he should, on leaving *Bellerophon,* wish to refer once more to a matter for which he bore such great responsibility. He therefore sought a last interview with Maitland. But Maitland lost patience, and the conversation degenerated into an altercation, of which Lord Keith chanced to hear a few exchanges. Las Cases, much agitated, tried to blame Lord Keith himself, but was sharply rebuked.

However, the Admiral, anxious not to have the matter on his conscience, and thinking there was nothing to lose by going further into the circumstances of the surrender, decided to ask his subordinate for additional information. He received Maitland's final report on 8 August, just when *Northumberland* was about to sail. Having read it, Lord Keith considered that Maitland's explanations were satisfactory, and allowed the ship to proceed.

On 10 August he wrote to the First Lord of the Admiralty:

Ville de Paris in Hamoaze,
10th August, 1815.

My Lord,

   Count de Las Cases having in an interview that I granted him on the morning of the 7 inst. on board the *Tonnant* asserted that when he was on board the *Bellerophon* in Basque Roads on a mission from General Buonaparte Captain Maitland informed him that he was authorized to receive the General and his suite on board that ship for conveyance to England, and that him and them [sic] would be well received there, I considered it right to apprise Captain Maitland of these assertions and to direct him to state for my information, and that of His Majesty's Government, any observations he might deem it expedient to make on them.

   A copy of this report I have the honour to enclose, attested by Captain Gambier of the *Myrmidon,* so far as he was present at the conversation referred to, and I have no doubt that a similar attestation will be made by Captain Sartorius of the *Slaney* as soon as he returns into port.

   It is due to Captain Maitland that I should add that while on board the *Bellerophon* on the forenoon of the 7th instant I heard a part of the conversation that passed upon the subject between him

and Count de Las Cases, by which it appeared to me that the latter
by no means established the truth of the assertions which he had
made.

   I have the honour to be, etc.

KEITH
Admiral

The report Maitland rendered in accordance with his instructions
was in these terms:

H.M.S. Bellerophon,
Plymouth Sound,
8th August, 1815.

My Lord,
  I have to acknowledge the receipt of your Lordship's letter of
yesterday's date, informing me that Count Las Cases had stated to
you that he had understood from me when he was on board the
Bellerophon in Basque Roads, on a mission from General Buonaparte,
that I was authorized to receive the General and his suite on board
the ship I command, for a conveyance to England, and that I
assured him at the same time, that both the General and his suite
would be well received there; and directing me to report for your
Lordship's information such observations as I may consider it
necessary to make upon these assertions. I shall, in consequence,
state, to the best of my recollection, the whole of the transaction
that took place between Count Las Cases and me, on the 14 July,
respecting the embarkation of Napoleon Buonaparte, for the
veracity of which I beg to refer your Lordship to Captain Sartorius[1]
as to what was said in the morning, and to that officer and Captain
Gambier[2] (the *Myrmidon* having joined me in the afternoon) as to
what passed in the evening.
  Your Lordship being informed already of the flag of truce that
came out to me on the 10 July, as well as of everything that occurred
on that occasion, I shall confine myself to the transactions of the
14th of the same month.
  Early in the morning of that day, the officer of the watch informed me a schooner, bearing a flag of truce, was approaching;

---

[1] Robert Sartorius (1790–1885). Present at Trafalgar and the actions of the
River Plate and Montevideo. Commanded the small ship *Slaney* in 1815.
Entered the service of the young Queen of Portugal in 1831, and defended her
against the pretender Don Miguel. She conferred on him the title of Count.
Promoted Admiral in 1861.
 [2] Robert Gambier (1791–1872). Nephew of Admiral Gambier. From 1804
onwards took part in several campaigns. In 1815 commanded the small sloop
Myrmidon under Maitland. Captain 1832; Admiral 1862.

on her joining the ship, about 7.00 a.m. the Count Las Cases and General Lallemand came on board, when, on being shown into the cabin, Las Cases asked me if any answer had been returned to the letter sent by me to Sir Henry Hotham respecting Napoleon Buonaparte being allowed to pass for America, either in the frigates, or in a neutral vessel. I informed him no answer had been returned, though I hourly expected, in consequence of these despatches, Sir Henry Hotham would arrive; and as I had told Monsieur Las Cases when last on board, that I should send my boat in when the answer came, it was quite unnecessary to send out a flag of truce on that account; there, for the time the conversation terminated. On their coming on board, I had made the signal for the Captain of the Slaney, being desirous of having a witness to all that might pass.

After breakfast (during which Captain Sartorius came on board) we retired to the after-cabin, when Monsieur Las Cases began on the same subjects and said, 'The Emperor was so anxious to stop the further effusion of blood, that he would go to America in any way the English Government would sanction, either in a neutral, a disarmed frigate, or an English ship of war'. To which I replied, 'I have no authority to permit any of these measures, but if he chooses to come on board the ship I command, I think, under the orders I am acting with, I may venture to receive him and carry him to England; but if I do so, I can in no way be answerable for the reception he may meet with (this I repeated several times); when Las Cases said, 'I have little doubt, under those circumstances, that you will see the Emperor on board the *Bellerophon*'. After some more general conversation, and the above being frequently repeated, Monsieur Las Cases and General Lallemand took their leave: and I assure your Lordship that I never, in any way, entered into conditions with respect to the reception General Buonaparte was to meet with; nor was it, at that time, finally arranged that he was to come on board the *Bellerophon*. In the course of conversation, Las Cases asked me whether I thought Buonaparte would be well received in England, to which I gave the only answer I could do in my situation – That I did not at all know what was the intention of the British Government, but I had no reason to suppose he would not be well received. It is here worthy of remark that when Las Cases came on board, he assured me that Buonaparte was then at Rochefort, and that it would be necessary for him to go there to report the conversation that had passed between us (this I can prove by the testimony of Captain Sartorius and the First Lieutenant of this ship, to whom I spoke of it at the time) which statement was not fact; Buonaparte never having quitted Isle d'Aix, or the frigates after the 3rd.

I was, therefore, much surprised at seeing Monsieur Las Cases on board again before seven o'clock the same evening; and one of the first questions I put to him was, whether he had been at Rochefort. He answered, that on returning to Isle d'Aix, he found that Buonaparte had arrived there.

Monsieur Las Cases then presented to me the letter Count Bertrand wrote concerning Buonaparte's intention to come on board the ship (a copy of which has been transmitted to your Lordship by Sir Henry Hotham), and it was not till then agreed upon that I should receive him; when either Monsieur Las Cases, or General Gourgaud (I am not positive which as I was employed writing my own despatches) wrote to Bertrand to inform him of it. While paper was preparing to write the letter, I said again to Monsieur Las Cases 'You will recollect I have no authority for making conditions of any sort'. Nor has Monsieur Las Cases ever started such an idea till the day before yesterday. That it was not the feeling of Buonaparte or the rest of his people, I will give strong proof drawn from the conversations they have held with me.

As I never heard the subject mentioned till two days ago, I shall not detail every conversation that has passed, but confine myself to that period.

The night that the squadron anchored at the back of Berry Head, Buonaparte sent for me about 10 p.m. and said he was informed by Bertrand that I had received orders to remove him to the *Northumberland,* and wished to know if that was the case; on being told that it was, he requested I would write a letter to Bertrand, stating I had such orders, that it might not appear that he went of his own accord, but that he had been forced to do so. I told him, I could have no objection, and wrote a letter to that effect (a copy of which is here annexed) which your Lordship afterwards sanctioned, and desired me, if he required it, to give him a copy of the order.

After having arranged that matter, I was going to withdraw, when he requested me to remain as he had something more to say; he then began complaining of his treatment in being forced to go to St Helena; among other things, he observed, 'They say I made no conditions; certainly I made no conditions; how could a private man (*un particulier*) make conditions with a nation? I wanted nothing from them but hospitality, or (as the ancients would express it) air and water, I threw myself on the generosity of the English nation; I claimed a place *sur leurs foyers*, and my only wish was to purchase a small estate, and end my life in tranquillity'. After more of the same sort of conversation, I left him for the night.

On the morning he removed from the *Bellerophon* to the *Northumberland,* he sent for me again, and said, 'I have sent for you to express my gratitude for your conduct to me, while I have been on board the ship you command. My reception in England has been very different from what I expected; but you throughout have behaved like a man of honour; and I request you will accept my thanks, as well as convey them to the officers, and ship's company of the *Bellerophon*.'

Soon afterwards Montholon came to me from Buonaparte; but to understand what passed between him and me, I must revert to a conversation that I had with Mme Bertrand on the passage from Rochefort.

It is not necessary to state how the conversation commenced, as it does not apply to the present transaction; but she informed me that it was Buonaparte's decision to present me with a box containing his picture set with diamonds. I answered, 'I hope not, for I cannot receive it'. 'Then you will offend him very much', she said. 'If that is the case', I replied, 'I request you will take measures to prevent its being offered, as it is absolutely impossible I can accept it; and I wish to spare him the mortification, and myself the pain, of a refusal'. There the matter dropt, and I heard no more of it, till about half an hour before Buonaparte quitted the *Bellerophon,* when Montholon came to me, and said he was desired by Buonaparte to express the high sense he entertained of my conduct throughout the whole of the transaction; that it had been his intention to present me with a box containing his portrait, but that he understood I was determined not to accept it. I said, 'Placed as I was, I felt it impossible to receive a present from him, though I was highly flattered at the testimony he had borne to the uprightness of my conduct throughout'. Montholon then added, 'One of the greatest causes of chagrin he feels in not being admitted to an interview with the Prince Regent, is that he had determined to ask as a favour your being promoted to the rank of Rear Admiral'. To which I replied 'That would have been quite impossible, but I do not the less feel the kindness of the intention'. I then said, 'I am hurt that Las Cases should say I held out any assurances as to the reception Buonaparte was to meet with in England'. 'Oh', said he, 'Las Cases is disappointed in his expectation; and as he negotiated the affair, he attributes the Emperor's situation to himself; but I can assure you, that he (Buonaparte) feels convinced that you have acted as a man of honour throughout.'

As your Lordship overheard part of a conversation which took place between Las Cases and me on the quarter-deck of the *Bellerophon,* I shall not detail it; but on that occasion, I positively denied having promised anything as to the reception of Buonaparte and his suite; and I believe your Lordship was of opinion that he could not make out the statement to you.

It is extremely unpleasant for me to be under the necessity of entering into a detail of this sort; but the unhandsome representation Monsieur Las Cases has made to your Lordship of my conduct has obliged me to produce proofs of the light in which the transaction was viewed by Buonaparte as well as his attendants.

I again repeat that Captains Gambier and Sartorius can verify the principal part of what I have stated, as far as concerns the charge made against me by Count Las Cases.

> I have the honour to be,
> Your Lordship's
> Most obedient, humble servant
>   FREDERICK L. MAITLAND.

There were appended the signatures of Gambier, commanding the *Myrmidon,* and of Sartorius, commanding the *Slaney* (given after his return to harbour.)

At the same time as Maitland was bending over the oak table in his sea cabin, racing against time to comply with his superior's orders, another pen with other ink, influenced by considerations of quite a different kind, produced a draft document that would be read the world over. When he transferred to the *Northumberland,* anger consumed the Imperial soul. Napoleon had no intention while off the inhospitable coast of England of submitting tamely to adversity. Before leaving the *Bellerophon* he would somehow nail to the ship's mast his supreme protest against the fate that was in store for him, the protest of protests which, in impressive style, would contain the sum total of his grievances, disappointment and bitterness, a masterpiece of propaganda for his own time and for posterity:

I hereby solemnly protest, in the face of Heaven, and of man, against the violence done me, and against the violation of my most sacred rights, in forcibly disposing of my person and my liberty. I came voluntarily on board of the *Bellerophon*: I am not a prisoner, I am the guest of England. I came on board even at the instigation of the Captain who told me he had orders from the Government to receive me and my suite, and conduct me to England, if agreeable to me. I presented myself with good faith to put myself under the protection of the English laws. As soon as I was on board the *Bellerophon,* I was under the shelter of the British people.

If the Government, in giving orders to the Captain of the *Bellerophon* to receive me as well as my suite, only intended to lay a snare for me, it has forfeited its honour and disgraced its flag.

If this act be consummated, the English will in vain boast to Europe of their integrity, their laws, and their liberty: British good faith will be lost in the hospitality of the *Bellerophon*.

I appeal to History: it will say that an enemy, who for twenty years waged war against the English people, came voluntarily in his misfortunes, to seek an asylum under their laws. What more brilliant proof could he give of his esteem and his confidence? But what return did England make for so much magnanimity? They feigned to stretch forth a friendly hand to that enemy; and when he delivered himself up in good faith, they sacrificed him.

NAPOLEON

On board the *Bellerophon* 4 August 1815.

Such was the solemn protest of Napoleon which, in its taut and flowing style, recalled the most celebrated of the Imperial proclamations. But in his misfortune the Emperor deceived himself and deceived posterity. How could he maintain that he embarked in *Bellerophon* 'at the suggestion of Captain Maitland who had instructions to take him to England together with his retinue, if that was agreeable to the Emperor'? Maitland's orders contained nothing political. He was instructed that, in the event of the capture of Napoleon, he (Maitland) was *not* to take him to England, but only to an English port, there to await fresh instructions.

The fact was that Maitland, owing to a combination of circumstances, was involved in a situation not foreseen by the Admiralty, which had only envisaged the Emperor escaping in a warship or merchantman, in which case all possible measures would have to be taken to capture the fugitive. Now, as it turned out, there was no fugitive, and Maitland, who had not the benefit of wireless telegraphy, had to interpret his orders cannily, since his career might hang on his interpretation. His first step, concurred in by his superior Sir Henry Hotham, was to block the escape of the Emperor so that he would eventually have no alternative but to board the *Bellerophon*.

Napoleon had the shrewdness to realize that his surrender to the English would be a gambler's final throw of the dice—but the dice rebounded against the player. Not only chance, but the logic of events, was to allow no other outcome. After the escape from Elba and the Allies' joint declaration of March, 1815, it was, in effect, impossible for England, even if in a burst of generosity she wished to welcome Napoleon with open arms, to provide him with the sympathetic treatment accorded to Lucien Bonaparte. But sound though all these reasons were, it was not politic for Napoleon to advance them. For, at that time, the myth that the Emperor was trapped—fostered by friends such as Savary—would have been dissolved by the acid of reality and there would only have remained a prisoner without honour, instead of a hero deceived by the enemies in whom he had placed his trust. It is also reasonable to assume that Napoleon, naturally anxious to preserve his prestige, and in this probably supported by Las Cases (very anxious to shift the blame from himself), phrased his letter in the same spirit as he phrased the communiqués he used to send in the old days to the Imperial news-sheet, *Le Moniteur*.

Finally, it is curious to compare the attitude which Napoleon, in his famous letter, adopted for the benefit of world opinion, with the attitude he always adopted in private towards Captain Maitland, of whose conduct he did not at any time complain. The Emperor had a violent temper, which had led him into conflict with Talleyrand and Metternich in the past. It had also led him into trouble with the British Ambassador (Lord Whitworth), at the time of the rupture of the Peace of Amiens in 1803. Yet he never showed anger to Maitland, and indeed treated him with courtesy. The fact is that the Emperor, face to face with Maitland, could find no grounds for complaint. Maitland had nothing to answer for, but the situation required a culprit. His was one of the reputations that had to be sacrificed, to convince posterity that history was on Napoleon's side and that the future would see the rise of the Second Empire.

8

CHAPTER 11

To St Helena

The nobler action is in virtue than in vengeance.

SHAKESPEARE

THE 'BELLEROPHON' had arrived off Plymouth Sound on 24 July, and on 7 August the *Northumberland,* her refit and victualling barely completed and without her usual store of fresh water which she would have to take on at the Azores, prepared to sail for St Helena.

Just before sailing Napoleon had a visit from a member of the House of Lords, Lord Lowther, and a member of the House of Commons, Mr Neville Lyttelton. After the visit Mr Lyttelton made a few notes, which have survived. He watched Napoleon arriving in a pinnace, expressionless, his head larger than appeared from his portraits. Over his forehead his brown, almost sandy hair hung long and untidy. His expression was sharp, rather than lofty. His eyes which must once have been very keen were now haggard and a little drooping. Age had dimmed their fire. His lack-lustre complexion was that of a sick man.

On arriving on board Napoleon had an interview with Mr Lyttelton and once more protested against the treatment meted out to him. 'By imprisoning me as you have, you have stained the flag and honour of England'. 'No' answered Mr Lyttelton, 'we have broken no undertakings; the national interest requires that it be put out of your power to return to France.' 'Well, what you are doing may be politic, but not generous. You are behaving like a petty state, not like a great and free nation. I have come to seat myself at your hearth as a private citizen of England.' This was said in a flat, almost detached tone.

Mr Lyttelton objected that Napoleon had many supporters in France and that France was not far away. The Emperor replied: 'No, my career is ended. You should have relied on my word of honour: your conduct towards me is less than noble. History will be your judge.' Lyttelton retorted that in England, since his invasion of Spain, no one trusted the Emperor's word. The latter

then commented: 'If I had known what was to befall me, I would
rather have surrendered to Austria or Russia.' But Mr Lyttelton
did not attach much importance to that observation, since he was
aware that when Lord Keith had expressed the view that St Helena
was preferable to Russia Napoleon had answered 'God preserve
me from Russia'.

Mr Lyttelton's final observation was that only two Poles (one
of them probably Piontowski) displayed any emotion on the
departure of the Emperor, the Frenchmen he had chosen as
companions remaining inscrutable. He may be mistaken here, for
their distress was noted by Lord Keith and Maitland.

On 9 August the *Northumberland* with a N.W. wind set a westerly
course to clear the English Channel. It was on the 16 July that the
Emperor had embarked in *Bellerophon,* full of hope in the
magnanimity of the Prince Regent and the English people.
Disappointed at Plymouth following his appeal to a law that, as it
turned out, did not apply to him, Napoleon started the long voyage
that was to lead to his Calvary.

In addition to her ship's company and Napoleon and his retinue,
the *Northumberland* carried the officers and also two companies of
the 53rd Regiment of Foot, with a battery of artillery, as reinforce-
ments for the Island, in all about 1,060 persons. In a ship of 1,600
tons, the cramped conditions of her passengers during a voyage of
71 days can easily be imagined. The Emperor's cabin, the only one
he had to himself, measured about 21 feet by 15 feet. Its height
between decks was about 5 ft.,[1] or a little less than that of its
occupant. It was the best cabin on board. The courteous Maitland
was no longer in command, and Lord Keith's mission was ac-
complished. Admiral Sir George Cockburn was now responsible
for the Emperor. Cockburn was a dry, bearded old seaman, a
stickler for the Service, but he was also a man of some education.
After initial clashes he did his best, within the limits of his
instructions, to make the Emperor's voyage tolerable. Napoleon
was given the place of honour at table. On days when a heavy sea
was running the Admiral would offer his arm to the Emperor and

---

[1] These dimensions were identical with those of Napoleon's cabin in *Bellerophon,* but she had far fewer people on board and Napoleon had the use of a
second cabin. The author is indebted to the Historical Section of the British
Admiralty for this information.

guide him back to his cabin. Oddly enough, on some days Napoleon would ask the ship's band to play for him *God Save the King* and *Rule Britannia.*

To Lord Liverpool and his colleagues the sailing of the *Northumberland* brought great relief and the end of a period of great anxiety. The British Cabinet now felt secure. The great Emperor, the arch enemy, was now a prisoner for life. British ministers had no feelings of remorse, for they considered they had acted with humanity and in such a way that the Emperor's life was spared. (Far worse was to be the fate of Murat, shot in compliance with one of his own decrees.) To them St Helena was the only possible choice, since Europe was ruled out; any of the Continental countries could provide avenues for escape, and the United States would have been able to allow the Emperor a freedom of movement which might not be put to good use. In the British Government's view, Napoleon was still capable of carving out an Empire for himself there. At that very moment half-pay officers, proscribed Bonapartists, were about to leave for Texas with the intention of founding a 'Champ d'Asile,' on the as yet unmarked frontier and they would have been a rallying point for the Emperor's supporters. The enterprise was a failure owing to bad organization and shortage of funds. What, on the other hand, would have been Napoleon's fate if he had reached America and led the expedition?[1]

To confine Napoleon somewhere in England was unthinkable; the Tower of London was unfit for habitation; a strongly fortified castle like Dumbarton was too grim. To assign a place in the shires where the Emperor could act the squire would have been rash. England was too near France, which was too accessible and afforded too many chances of intrigue.

Furthermore, Napoleon was too great a personality to be reduced — as the American Indians reduced heads to the size of a fist — to the size of a simple private citizen of the name of Duroc or Muiron, living obscurely on his estate. The Liberal opposition might have rallied round him as much for political reasons to score a point off the Government as for reasons of principle and who knows what might have happened at such a juncture? The circumstances might have been favourable enough for a Bona-

[1] In 1816 two brothers, the Generals Lallemand, joined the movement, but they were of no assistance, being as incompetent administrators as they were brave soldiers.

partist nucleus to have formed, a Trojan horse in the very heart of England. And the Emperor's personal magnetism, irresistible when he chose to exercise it, would have been exercised to the full. This was not a childish fear. Had there not been the spectacle at Torbay and Plymouth of swarms of boats pressing, regardless of the guard-boats, towards the side of his ship? They were loaded with sightseers, attracted by curiosity like iron filings by a powerful magnet.

Lord Keith, for his part, thought that Napoleon, had he been allowed to see the Prince Regent, would have conquered him as he had conquered Alexander at Tilsit. If Napoleon had passed through London, who knows what a welcome he would have had from the crowds? In 1802, at the time of the ratification of the Treaty of Amiens, the crowds had detached the horses of General Lauriston so that they themselves could haul the carriage.

On board the *Northumberland* there were simple sailors who succumbed to the Imperial charm. They were sailing unwillingly —they had completed a foreign service commission and were due for leave—and although twenty hot-heads had been taken off the ship there were some on board who on the passage out went so far as to lay hands on the midshipmen. What would have happened if, taking advantage of this ill wind, the Emperor, who had cajoled the boatswain and had even invited him to his cabin, though he was not of officer rank—a favour which had rightly shocked the supercilious Cockburn as being against regulations—had engineered a mutiny on board, and having hoisted the tricolour set sail for another destination? An absurd theory, it may be said, but had not the meteoric career of the General, First Consul and Emperor been marked with the most extraordinary feats of audacity? We will admit, however, that the presence of two companies of Marines between decks would have allowed little chance of success for such an enterprise.

A man like this, without an army, without a crown, having lost his lands and liberty, remained, by reason of the glamour that still surrounded his person even in defeat, a real danger to his victors. He was always feared. He excited fear.

That is why, in the eyes of the British Cabinet, the solution arrived at, based as it was on these known considerations, was the only one that commended itself.

Those who were fanatical supporters of the Emperor, however, had by no means ceased to defend him. Capell Lofft was watching. In a second letter, even more biting than the first, he castigated those responsible for the grim future of Napoleon. On 10 August the *Morning Chronicle* bore the following letter under his signature:

> Truston Hall,
> Bury St Edmunds,
> Suffolk.

To The Editor of the *Morning Chronicle*.
> 'The nobler action is
> In virtue than in vengeance: he being here
> The sole drift of our purpose, wrath here ends;
> Not a frown further.'   *The Tempest*

Sir,

On this great subject, I shall recapitulate and enlarge. It has appeared that the Emperor of France had abdicated to remove the alleged ground of the war of the confederates again France: the abdicational condition was not adopted. The war still continuing, he takes another step. 'Having terminated his political career he comes, like Themistocles, to assure himself of the hospitality of the British people. He claims of His Royal Highness the Prince Regent the protection of the laws of England, and throws himself on the most powerful, the most constant, yet most generous of his enemies.' Two of these characteristics need no proof: the same might have been hoped of the third.

According to the best modern usuage and the nature of the subject, prisoners of war, unless sooner exchanged or ransomed, return to their country; or go elsewhere, at liberty, when the war is terminated. They are pledges not prizes in perpetuity. But a prisoner of war cannot be made after the war is over. A prisoner of war would be strangely made by voluntarily committing himself — on the part of the Chief on whose account war was waged — to the hospitality, generosity and laws of the State with whom he had been at war, but whom, after this act of his, he considered as enemies no longer. By Lord Castlereagh himself, it is considered as having terminated hostilities; and is it to be inoperative singly as to the illustrious individual whose act it is?

Mr Burdon, who is certainly not favourable to Bonaparte, to this great and wonderful man (wonderful he admits him to be), and who, I apprehend, is astonishingly and incalculably mistaken in supposing that whenever Bonaparte dies he will die unpitied and unregretted, yet conceives that 'both generosity and justice require

that he be forthwith set at liberty'. I have already stated the grounds
for the same opinion. Both he and I agree that by the law of nations
and of nature, there would be no difficulty as to this. But he thinks
there is a great difficulty because the confederates, with whom we
are allied, have acted wrong; and by so doing, have put themselves
under an extreme embarrassment how to act rightly. This embarrassment of theirs will be no justification either to them or to us;
and it can be no excuse for our disregarding the law of nations and
of nature, for our violating our own constitutional law, for our
disclaiming by act the high character and opinion of us on which
this heroic visitant has staked his all, esteeming us as incapable of
disappointing his confidence in our generosity and justice.

I have said too that if he were a prisoner of war under the most
favourable of all possible circumstances he ought to be regarded as
coming under his parole hither; not to be imprisoned on his arrival,
refused permission to land or see anyone, and consigned to
perpetual captivity (which is slavery), under guard of his enemies;
beyond the seas, in a remote, scarcely accessible and almost
deserted island. The idea of a prisoner at war to be excluded from
all release, ransom or exchange under any possible circumstances
(and the place designed confirms the statement that such was the
intention) is utterly repugnant to all principles and practice of
modern civilized war.

It does not follow that because prisoners of war brought to
England may be kept in England during the war, that therefore, as
the *Courier* supposes, they may be sent out of it prisoners for life;
beyond the pale of our laws and constitution. It does not follow
that, because by temporary statutes aliens may now be required
and compelled to quit this island when we are at war with their
country; therefore, when we are at peace with it, they coming and
claiming the protection of our laws, their claim is to be answered
by our sending them away prisoners by force and for ever.

I have stated that a foreigner, while in England, is a temporary
subject; this distinction between the *subdile perpetui et temporarii*
is recognized by Grotius and by our own jurists.

I have stated that, as such, owing to local allegiance, he is
entitled to protection while he stays with us; and that he is therefore within the full benefit of the Act of *Habeas Corpus*; and of this
there can be no doubt, either in principle or in practice.

But, now, a new method is started for rectifying all this accumu-
lated, unexampled wrong; wrong which ought to strike general
terror and alarm if committed against the most obscure individual.
And here pardon me, but I really distrusted my senses, and doubted
whether I was reading the *Morning Chronicle* or not rather *The Times*

or the *Courier*. A precedent has been found, and a line of conduct
is clearly marked out — 'By no means let the laws of England be
violated': but once clear of that all is well. A precedent! I should
have been astonished if one had been found. This, which our
Ministers have endeavoured to make (and if they can succeed, it will
serve for every and for any thing) this will resound through the
world, and through all history and all time. And I trust the fate of
it will effectually prevent there ever being such another.

But what is this precedent? Major John Bernardi, a Count of the
Empire, born in England, was apprehended on-board a ship lying
off Colchester, at low water mark, and committed under a warrant
of a justice, November, 1691; and afterwards by the Lords of the
Privy Council, and afterwards removed to close confinement in
Newgate, 25 March, 1696. There not being sufficient evidence
to try him, he and others were detained by an Act of 10 and 11
William III c. 13. King William, it is said, promised that he
would, in a short time, release him. He died — they remained in
custody.

By successive Acts of Parliament, this officer and nobleman,
Major Bernardi, was further detained in custody during the reigns
of Queen Anne and George I. He was reduced to a deplorable state
of suffering, by ulcers from a wound, and from his long confinement; having, as he stated in his petition to the Queen, suffered for
near thirty-two years a thousand-fold worse than a present violent
death. And at length, having been confined during the whole of
three reigns, within some few days, and during part of a fourth, he
was liberated, having suffered five years more after his being
reduced to the dreadful state described — liberated by death
in the 37th year from his first imprisonment (having been a short
time on bail, in the early part of it) and in the 82nd year of his
age.
Merciful Heaven! And are such things precedents? And is this
the way to honour the Statute Law of England? To make it a
precedent at all, Napoleon must have been shown to have conspired
since his coming to England against the Crown; or at least, to have
committed in England some great crime against the Government
of this country.

It is a precedent for nothing to show that charges for a violation
of the law of the land, committed by one in it and born in it, may be
the subject of imprisonment in order to trial; that the common law,
and the statute, till unduly changed, will not endure perpetual or
indefinite imprisonment; and that a vessel lying at low water mark
lies within the county to which the adjacent shore belongs.

But it is a precedent for a special act to transport Bonaparte for life. For what? For acts done when he held the supreme government in France, or for returning from Elba, of which the supreme Government was stipulated to him during life; to the Government of France to which he was again adopted? Do we fear, or can France expect, that he would return to it again?

Even the severe Grotius mitigates his interpretation of the then much less understood rights of war and peace than they are now understood. And by the 10th chapter of his Third Book, acknowledges that the *aequum et bonum*, the sense of justice and humanity and benevolence; the *pudor*, the shame of being ungenerous and cruel; and the prevalence of Christian morality have tacitly relinquished many supposed rights of war, which were rather precedents of fact than evidence of right. No custom, no precedent, no Act of Parliament, can give a right to do great and manifest and perpetual wrong.

But to what barbarism must we go for this, as a part of even the supposed laws of nations? We should still be the *Britanni hospitibus feri*, the Britons fierce and hostile to strangers visiting them, if we could still suffer it to be so considered in ours.

We can never make it a part of the right and fit and becoming; we can never reconcile it to our common law and constitution; we can never without just shame and eternal reproach, make it the subject of a statute of this realm of England.

By what title should we describe, what preamble give to it? An Act to transport for life as a prisoner beyond the seas to St Helena Napoleon Bonaparte, more than twenty years Emperor of France, he having voluntarily come to Great Britain, claiming the protection of our laws, assuring himself of our hospitality, and throwing himself on the justice and generosity of the British people.

Mark, I beseech, how this becomes the House! If we intended to make the name of an Act of Parliament odious and ridiculous and synonymous with the extreme of folly, injustice and cruelty; then, and then only, such an Act might be proposed and imagined possible to pass the two Houses, and receive the sanction of the Crown. Can we be yet to learn that it is not law that makes justice, but justice that alone constitutes law?

But Ministers are to have an indemnity—an indemnity!—sprouts (*sic*) of Savile, of Fox and of Whitbread; and I might add Pitt, father and son; spirit of Nelson; and thou living-genius of our armies, and thou aged King, in whose name and behalf thy son, the Prince Regent, administers the Government—an indemnity;—for what?

When a clear general necessary good has been done under circumstances that could not wait for the sanction of Parliament, and which could not legally be done without it, there an indemnity is of right: where an error has been incurred in nice and subordinate points of administration, but not against any clear general principles of the constitution, not against the law of nations or of nature, and the national character; there an indemnity is admissible. But an indemnity for transporting this most illustrious of visitants — thus coming, thus confiding himself to us and who by his arrival has terminated the war — imprisoning him immediately for the purpose of transporting him for life to St Helena! If for this an indemnity is to be had, or even asked, I know not for what deeds it may be challenged and obtained for the time to come.

But 'we must know whatever is indispensible to the public security'. Doubtless, but against whom? Against him who places himself, if we will consent, under our laws; against him who trusts to the English government and nation; against him and about fifty of his faithful and honourable friends, including their wives and children? Indispensible security to the Crown and Parliament of England; to the Duke of Wellington and army of Waterloo; to our navy and to twelve million of British inhabitants? Would a single individual feel right such security in the imprisonment of another individual for life? and shall such a conduct be imagined indispensible to the security of this high-spirited, free and great nation? What is indispensible in this? — to do justice, to practise benevolence, and to fear nothing while we adhere to these.

Other ideas have been started, which it would be a libel on the country and the Government to suppose can be meant; such as seizing the library, so far as it remains, of Bonaparte, and his other property which he brought with him hither; and such as sending the Generals Bertrand and Lallemand, proscribed by the present Government of France (by Fouché and Talleyrand) prisoners thither, to the disposal of the Government. It ought not to be believed that this will ever be.

I conclude thus: that perfect liberty to Bonaparte and his faithful friends, who have accompanied him to reside, if he and they shall be so inclined, here in freedom, would be the just and true policy, perfectly secure and honourable; that to transport him hence beyond the seas prisoner for life, or deliver any of them to their enemies, would be a violation of all law, all principle, and all policy, from which our law can and ought to protect him and them.

I am, Sir, yours,

CAPEL LOFFT.

Capell Lofft's appeal was soon criticized by an influential Tory paper of the day, *The Courier*. Its leading article for 20 August,

1815, gave short shift to Liberal generosity and delivered a crushing rejoinder on Napoleon:

We have published Buonaparte's protest against being sent to St Helena. That he should remain to the last totally regardless of truth will not surprise anyone. He protests 'against the violation of his most sacred rights, by the forcible disposal of his person and property, for he came freely on board the *Bellerophon*, and was not the prisoner but the guest of England'. When he found he could not escape to America, and that he was in danger of being carried back to Paris, he surrendered himself to us — But in what way? First, he wanted to make conditions to be permitted to pass freely on his way to America (to which country, it is now said, he sent immense sums before the battle of Waterloo): this was refused — to be permitted to reside at liberty in England: this was also denied him. Captain Maitland told him expressly that he could only receive him as a prisoner surrendering unconditionally, though we have heard it reported that he added his personal safety would, no doubt, be assured. So that Buonaparte did give himself into our hands without any condition beyond that of having his life spared. Did he suppose for a moment that after having violated the treaty which gave him Elba we shall suffer him to be at large in this kingdom not more than twenty-five miles from the French coast? Why, he must have thought that the members of the Opposition were in Administration, for none but they would be guilty of such folly. In them, and in his other eulogists in this country, this protest will create great sympathy and pity. What harsh treatment of 'the greatest of all living men!' And yet these admirers of a military tyrant are clamourers for liberty. So it is with the Democrats of America and the Jacobins of France. What inference can possibly be drawn from this, but that their love of liberty is pretence and hollow hypocrisy? It is not liberty that they want, but a tyranny of which they shall themselves participate; and any man is with them a hero, and a god, by whose aid they might trample the rest of the world under their feet. But British laws are for British protection, not for the protection of our deadly enemies. They protect the oppressed, not the oppressor; and they will not throw their shield over the object of Jacobin tenderness and idolatry. What is the wish of these men? They would prevent his being sent abroad; would they then have him kept a closer prisoner at home? No such thing; they would have him at liberty, unchained, unprisoned, stalking abroad to receive their homage, and glittering in the spoils of his robberies. Were he even in prison here, they would, we suppose, take their regular morning lounge at his prison gate, with transport inhale the breezes that should pass over his cell, and fancy inspirations from his proximity. No, no; let his admirers have a longer journey for their gratification; let them make a pilgrimage to the prison of their prophet at St Helena, and there increase the still acknowledged 'child and champion of Jacobinism.'

These two samples from the press of the day sum up exactly the opposing English attitudes to the fallen sovereign. Their divergence and contrast could not but be surprising to younger French people who had only known the revolutionary gazettes and the sophisticated Imperial censorship.

Imagine the situation in reverse, and some fallen English Napoleon at the mercy of victorious France; the *Courier's* line would, in all probability, have been the only possible one to take. An opposite view would have been unthinkable.

That two opposing movements could arise in England was due to the fact that that country had for long been the land of liberty where anyone, provided that he did not contravene public order and morality, could express his opinion publicly and without restraint, whether it was conventional or not.

As well as this, the English drew from their history and their environment a marked disposition towards public debate rather than one-sided oratory and peremptory statement of a single point of view. Withal there is a willingness to listen patiently to the other side—characteristics that have hardly changed to this day. This can be seen in the physical layout of the House of Commons and the House of Lords, where views are tested and discussed from facing benches; on one side the Tories—the out-and-out conservatives—and on the other the advocates of change. The same concept also prevails in the court-room, where cases have been decided from time immemorial, as the saying goes, not after impassioned pleas but rather from the spark of truth raised by the clash of examination and cross-examination.

It may also be that the traditional pattern of team games and of school life, where opponents are ranged on opposite sides, has fostered this attitude and introduced into public life, besides certain rules like fair play, this willingness to hear both sides, which is less in evidence in other countries where overbearing passion carries the day. Not that the English are immune from passion; far from it—they are capable of great passion in politics, war, religion, and the emotions—but the difference is that even in the most hard-fought battles and bitter conflicts they understand passions in their adversaries.

However, there is another aspect of the English mentality which goes with what we have just said. That is, self-control in moments of anger, bitterness and grief; magnanimity towards their enemy in the moment of victory, even though they themselves may be dripping blood and sweat; thus the enemy though vanquished is not utterly crushed. At a time so exceptional as the summer of 1815, this instinct could understandably not have been in evidence, yet it still manifested itself; witness the champions of the cause who were able to try conclusions with official harshness and its supporters. All this is reflected in the popular sporting attitude of sympathy for the man who is down, the under-dog, as he is called. Two dogs fight; the loser is the under-dog. The Englishman will take the part of the weaker one, and getting the stronger by the ears, will prevent him from gaining complete victory. Humanitarian feeling throbs in the insular heart. Did not this humanitarian feeling lead to the abolition of slavery and legislation against cruelty to animals?

These few comments may assist the reader — at least, we hope they may — to appreciate better the two opposing viewpoints of the public in regard to the unfortunate prisoner, with his friends and enemies fighting against time in a final struggle, oblivious of the inexorability of fate.

The pro-Napoleon faction, ignorant of British traditions and watching the struggle with interest, were under a delusion as to its real implications and the influence of those who had taken the Emperor's side. The two sides, indulging in these public recriminations designed either to crush or save him, were too unequal.

The French hopefully compared Capell Lofft's articles on the one hand, and those in the *Courier* and other journals of the same political colour on the other. But such hopes were futile. On paper, and in theory, the arguments of both sides had equal force: but there was only a small audience for the Emperor's platform; whilst the circulation of the Tory journals was overwhelmingly in the majority, and they supported a Government whose actions they approved. The French had suddenly found themselves plunged into strange surroundings where free discussion prevailed; they were misled by a display of arguments and appeals intended to be rousing, but which failed to be heard effectively in a country alienated by imperial ventures, and obsessed by fear of further attack; a country that was ready to adopt the severest measures in the interests of its future defence.

CHAPTER 12

In Extremis

'Tis done – but yesterday a king,
And armed with kings to strive –
And now thou art a nameless thing :
An object – yet alive.
The Desolator desolate,
The Victor overthrown,
The Arbiter of others' fate
A suppliant for his own.

BYRON

WHEN NAPOLEON arrived at St Helena on 17 October the world thought that his fate was finally sealed. So, in point of fact, it was. The British Government, however, having all along entertained doubts as to the strict legality of the measures it had taken in regard to the fallen monarch, although it had the support of Lord Eldon's opinion, decided to ask Parliament to pass an Act of Indemnity which would absolve it of any illegality and ratify its policy. That action was to be taken with the utmost despatch. The Long Vacation did not impede the diligent activities of the Prime Minister and his legal advisers. Lord Eldon, shooting partridge on his estate at Encombe (perched – thanks to his short legs – on a Shetland pony) continually mulled over Napoleon's case, and on 16 September wrote to his brother, Sir William Scott, that he had not so far found a satisfactory answer to the problems of Buonaparte's case, had not felt able as yet to affix his seal to the Convention between the Allies, signed at Paris; and that not everybody was favourable to the Convention. He believed that they must have an Act of Indemnity to settle the question as far as possible.

On 4 October Lord Eldon wrote again to Sir William Scott:

> The result, however, seems to me to be that, in your judgment, Buonaparte is a French subject, and ought to have been so treated, by being delivered up to his sovereign. Now the misfortune is, that I apprehend that (the state of things in France considered) no one of the Allies would have listened for a moment to his being delivered up – (to continue in life) – to that sovereign, either to

127

remain in France, or, in his custody, in any other part of the world. Those who act upon politics and the main chance would never have consented to Buonaparte's being retained in life in French custody anywhere.

He goes on: 'Party I don't mind much; posterity not a great deal; for, of this transaction, in all its particulars, it will be as little informed in matter of fact as it is in most others;—but, to do the thing that is right, is really a matter of most anxious concern with me.'

On 1 October, the Prime Minister, Lord Liverpool, having received various other communications from Lord Eldon, replied:

> *Fife House,*
> *Oct. 1st, 1815.*

My dear Lord,
    I have read and considered your argument respecting the situation of Buonaparte, and think there is great weight in it. I own that I was inclined to think the Master of the Rolls' view of the question correct, that you had your choice of considering him (Buonaparte) either as a French subject, or as a captain of free-booters or banditti, and consequently out of the pale of the protec-tion of nations. Before he quitted Elba, he enjoyed only a limited and conditional sovereignity, which ceased when the condition on which he held it was violated. In which character, then, did he make war on the King of France, our ally? Not as an independent sovereign, for he had no such character: not as a pretender to the crown of France in any admissible sense, for he had absolutely and entirely renounced all claim of this description. He must then revert to his original character, of a French subject, or he has no character at all, and headed his expedition as an outlaw and outcast; *hostis humani generis.* I am quite clear that in whatever way the subject is viewed, it will be desirable to have an Act of Parliament to settle any doubts which may arise on such a question; but I trust we have one good ground to found it upon, if not two.

And so it was to be.

When it re-assembled, the House of Commons gave its attention to a Government Bill of Indemnity as well as a subsidiary Bill to regulate the steps that it would be desirable to take to guard Napoleon effectively. It was approved, *nemine contradicente*, only a few liberals abstaining.

The following is a précis of the two Acts. The principal Bill is entitled *An Act designed to ensure the safekeeping of Napoleon Bonaparte*:

Whereas it is essential for the peace and safety of Europe that Bonaparte should be detained as provided below. His Majesty the King, with the advice and consent of the Lords Spiritual and Temporal, and the Commons duly assembled, gives his royal sanction to the Promulgation of the following decrees:

i. It shall be lawful for His Majesty, his heirs and successors to commit the charge of the said Napoleon Bonaparte to such persons, and in such a place, and under such restraints as His Majesty, his heirs and successors see fit.

ii. The said Napoleon Bonaparte shall be detained as long as His Majesty, his heirs and successors shall direct, and it shall be lawful for them, under the seal of one of the principal Secretaries of State, to entrust the said Napoleon Bonaparte to any person they deem suitable, who shall be a subject of the Crown; and furthermore it shall be lawful for them, if it be deemed necessary, to convey the said Napoleon Bonaparte to some other place of detention, and to have authority to request the assistance of any other person or persons, these persons, moreover, being authorized to take all necessary precautions to guard the said Napoleon Bonaparte, and to recapture him if he contrives to escape.

iii. Furthermore, it is decreed that whosoever, being a British subject, shall be instrumental to the escape of Napoleon Bonaparte, or shall be an accessory to any attempt to assist him to transgress the limits assigned him, whether island, territory, or other place, whether upon parole or no, is guilty of a capital crime, and shall suffer death, without being able to claim benefit of clergy.

iv. Furthermore it is decreed that whosoever, being a British subject, shall offer aid or assistance to the said Napoleon Bonaparte after his violation of the bounds assigned him, whether upon parole or no, shall be held to have been a party to his escape in the sense of the present Act.

v. Furthermore, it is decreed that whosoever, being a British subject, shall, after the escape of Napoleon Bonaparte from his place of detention and his removal to some other country, or upon the high seas, bring help to the said Napoleon Bonaparte to consummate his flight, shall be guilty of a capital crime and shall suffer death without being able to claim benefit of clergy.

vi. Warning is also given that information may be laid of any infringement within the scope of this Act, wherever it may be committed, whether at home, or abroad, or at sea, and the culprit

9

brought to trial before a jury in any county of His Majesty's realm of England, exactly as if the said infringement had been committed in that country.

VII. Any person who shall be arrested or imprisoned under the terms of the present Act, may be sent to England for trial.

This Act is dated 11 April in the fifty-sixth year of the reign of George III.

The title and provisions of the supplementary Bill are as follows:

An Act to regulate communications with the Island of St Helena during such time as Napoleon be detained there.

Given that the said Napoleon Bonaparte is now detained upon the Island of St Helena, *Given* that it is essential to forbid any communication with the aforementioned island, either by subjects of His Majesty or by any other persons (with exception as under) so long as the detention of Napoleon may last, His Majesty, upon the advice and with the consent of the Lords Spiritual and Temporal, and the Commons duly assembled, gives his royal sanction to the promulgation of the present Act.

I. So long as Napoleon is a prisoner, no subject of His Majesty nor any other person may land upon St Helena (unless he be an employee of the East India Company) without the express authorization of His Majesty, duly signed by one of the Secretaries of State, or by permission of the Governor of the Island, or the officer commanding the naval and military forces on the island. Any person contravening these measures will be held to have committed a criminal act or misdemeanour, and may be brought before the Court of King's Bench upon the suit of the Attorney General, as if the act had been committed within his jurisdiction, and shall be subject to a term of imprisonment, or a fine, or such other penalty as the Court may decide, the present Act superseding any other law, statute or precedent.

II. Any person contravening these measures shall be apprehended and brought to England to stand trial, and shall be kept there, either under arrest or on bail, until the time when he shall be summoned before the Court of King's Bench.

III. Any person disembarking, whether from a ship of the aforementioned East India Company, or from one of His Majesty's ships (the crew excepted) and failing to return on board in defiance of the orders of the Governor, or his representatives, shall be arrested and detained by the authorities of the Island, or sent back to his ship; and any person who fails to return to his ship and remains on the Island, shall be held to be guilty of a misdemeanour, and dealt with in the same manner as those persons who land without permission.

IV. The Governor of St Helena, the Deputy Governor, or the officer commanding the naval and military forces, shall have the right to prevent, by every means in his power, any vessel from entering the harbour of the Island, whether for the purpose of transacting business or making repairs, or of effecting contact with the shore, saving the ships of the East India Company, and the aforesaid persons shall be enjoined to seize any person contravening the present disposition.

It is further laid down that any ship belonging wholly or in part to a British subject (except those described above) which shall be found cruising less than eight nautical miles from St Helena, shall be hailed and boarded in the name of His Majesty; and brought to England, where her owners shall be deemed to be subject to British jurisdiction, and shall be brought before the Court.

Furthermore, if the ship in question is flying a foreign flag and fails to comply with the injunction of the authorities on St Helena to keep her distance, the said vessel shall be treated as if she belonged to a British subject, and her owner proceeded against.

V. If, in spite of everything, a ship shall touch at St Helena, on account of the hazards of the sea, storms or for any other urgent reason, she may stay there during such time as necessary for her needs, on condition that she informs the authorities, and that her captain obeys all such instructions as he shall receive, the onus being upon him to establish his good faith. After which, the said vessel may freely depart.

VI. And should it happen that the Government, or other officials or authorities shall commit, for the better safe-keeping of Napoleon Bonaparte, acts which are not strictly legal, it shall be expedient to relieve them, or any others who may have assisted them, of responsibility by an Act of Indemnity which is hereby provided by the present legislation.[1]

VII. Moreover, all actions and suits which may have been made against the authorities responsible for such acts before the promulgation of the present Act, shall be suspended and declared null and void.

VIII. It should be made clear that the present dispositions shall not prevent the East India Company from enjoying its rights of commerce and navigation except when the exercise of these rights shall be irreconcilable with the present dispositions.

[1] This provision is the most surprising and unusual, as an Act of Indemnity cannot normally be prospective.

In April, 1816, the Bill was passed by the Commons and went to the Lords for approval. One of the most important motions was that of Lord Holland, that it was in the public interest that His Majesty's Judges attend a full session of the House so that their opinion[1] could be obtained on the following points:

1. What is meant in law by 'enemy alien'?
2. Can any person who is not an 'enemy alien' be detained as a prisoner of war?
3. Has an 'enemy alien', taken prisoner in wartime and held prisoner for the duration of hostilities, any right to a writ of *Habeas Corpus* from the moment a peace treaty is signed with the country of which he is a national, even if the peace treaty says nothing about the exchange or release of prisoners?
4. In law, again, can anyone be detained and treated as an 'enemy alien' if he is not the subject or ruler of any country?
5. Is it legal to treat anyone as an 'enemy alien' if the King of England is not at war with another country?
6. Can a prisoner of war conduct an action in the English courts against a British subject? If not, is this because he is a prisoner of war, or because he is the subject of a state with which the King of England is at war?

This motion was opposed by Lord Eldon, not so much on the ground that the questions were not reasonable, but principally because the Judges' answers would confuse the peers. It must be remembered what difficulty Lord Eldon found in reducing to a common denominator the various opinions he had gathered. It would be better, his opinion having prevailed, not to risk new controversies while an Act of Indemnity was being voted on.

During the debate that followed, Lord Holland rose and delivered a moving speech. This was its most important passage:

I shall not vote for the present Bill of Indemnity. To consign to distant exile and imprisonment a foreign and captive chief, who, after the abdication of his authority, relying on British generosity, had surrendered himself to us instead of his other enemies, is unworthy of the magnanimity of a great country—and the treaties by which, after his captivity, we bound ourselves to detain him in custody at the will of sovereigns to whom he had never surrendered himself, appear to me repugnant to the principles of equity, and utterly uncalled for by expedience or necessity.

[1] This procedure (now abolished) was still resorted to then in serious cases, as when a peer was accused of high treason.

Lord Castlereagh, speaking for the Government, urged the Lords to adopt the wording already passed by the Commons. His argument was elementary. He said that there were those who were doubtful of the Crown's right to hold Napoleon prisoner after hostilities had ceased. For his part, he held no such doubts, and in any case the present Bill was designed to put an end to them. That this policy was best, was not contested, while from a legal stand-point he felt it was entirely justified. The intention was to keep under strict guard the ex-sovereign of Elba, who was guilty of bad faith in making his escape. In general, it was of vital importance to ensure the public safety and the peace of the world.

After the debate, replying for the Government, Lord Castlereagh said finally that Napoleon Bonaparte would be treated as a prisoner of war and at all times with the greatest consideration.

Augustus Frederick, Duke of Sussex, brother of the Prince Regent, intervened to emphasize in the clearest and most courageous manner his opposition to the Bill of Indemnity, declaring that he could not approve of it any more than could Lord Holland.

In the end the Lords — without a division, in accordance with the practice of the Upper House — passed the Bill, which received the Royal Assent and became law.

Thereafter the British Government had liberty of action, and no one in England was able to question in any way the expediency, the merits or the legality of any steps taken in regard to Napoleon. Ministers could no longer be accused of having exceeded their powers. They were protected by this legislation. The subsidiary Bill was passed without debate.

Their prisoner being defenceless, the British Government could have mitigated the rigours of his transportation. But they did nothing of the kind. Lord Bathurst, Minister of War and Colonies, who was responsible for St Helena, was not the man to be moved by the sight of cruel misfortune, nor one to think of arranging for any relief; which, without endangering the Powers, could be afforded on moral and practical grounds, and even in the interest of the good name of England. He was moreover, to display a singular lack of judgment in appointing as Governor of St Helena a man most unfitted for the post. He sent out a warder when he should have sent a gentleman (one who did his duty, certainly, but

a gentleman). Again, how melancholy it is to have to record that
Hudson Lowe, to an unhealthy degree the slave of his instructions,
had not the sense to stretch a point, particularly as he was
thousands of miles from the authors of those instructions.

Nelson at Copenhagen, wishing to disregard the flagship's
signal, put his telescope to the eye he lost at Calvi. But Hudson
Lowe was no Nelson. Why did he obstinately refuse to address
Napoleon as 'Emperor'? He was, indeed, acting according to his
instructions, but what was there to prevent a tactful governor
uttering under his breath this title, so pleasing to the ear of
Napoleon, to make chivalrous gestures, to create a climate where
it would have been possible for the prisoner to move about without
unnecessary restraints, thus removing causes of irritation? Again,
why, instead of a rat-infested hovel, about which Napoleon with
understandable pride did not complain, was he not housed
decently in the East India Company's house—he who had had
Europe at his feet, frequented the Tuileries, Fontainebleau,
Schönbrunn, Potsdam and the Kremlin? The objection was that
this house was not suitable for surveillance. Why not build
another? These things are the substance of the criticism—not of
the punishment, which was unavoidable—but of its application,
of its manner, as Lord Rosebery put it. As Thiers wrote:

> Napoleon had risked the perils of surrendering to the British...
> But our quite natural French tendency to sympathize with our
> companion of the days of our glory should not make us lose sight
> of a self-evident fact, namely, that Europe, having been turned
> upside down over twenty years, and only fresh from the disturb-
> ance of her peace and the shedding of her blood in torrents, had to
> protect herself against new ventures, always a possibility where
> this bold genius was concerned. If he had only been a deposed
> monarch of but ordinary ability, like Louis XVIII, the rules of
> hospitality would have dictated that Napoleon be allowed to
> choose, in the freedom of England, a place where he could have
> ended his days. But to permit the man who had escaped from
> Elba, and drawn the arms of Europe on to the fields of Ligny and
> Waterloo, to roam the streets of London was out of the question.

Later, Thiers writes: 'Anything not necessary to prevent a second
escape would be a gratuitous cruelty that would weigh on the
conscience of those responsible.' And again, 'Detaining Napoleon
did not confer the right to torment him, nor to shorten his life, nor,

above all, to humiliate him. To respect his genius was a duty as
important as the right to restrain him.'

Certainly, with the passage of time, the judgments which
successive generations have passed on the treatment of the
Emperor at St Helena have been more and more severe. One can
see, and that more clearly nowadays, what the attitude of the
victors should have been. But, after the trials they had endured,
how could one expect them not to adopt an implacable attitude?
The war, with its great loss of life, had lasted twenty years; the
dead of Waterloo had just been buried. On the whole, English
public opinion leaned against showing pity or pardon, and saw
nothing repulsive in the act of retaliation. The representatives of
the allied commissioners at St Helena, who saw what was going
on, were of little use, and in London Lady Holland's views did not
gain acceptance. The Tsar was no longer the friend of the Tilsit
period. The Emperor of Austria no longer behaved like a father-
in-law, and Marie-Louise, separated from the man who had placed
the Imperial Crown on her head, came and went between Parma
and Rome, escorted by the one-eyed but handsome Neipperg.
Louis XVIII had but one object, to be sure of the throne of
which he was the legitimate heir and of which he had been
deprived by the usurper. That it was the ruthless energy of
Napoleon that had restored order to the Church and the State
after the Revolution now counted for little. '*Vae victis.*'
    Where does the truth lie? What were the rights of the matter?
What is just and true in one situation may not be so in another.
As long ago as 1840, a great English lawyer, Lord Campbell,[1] with
that lucidity and judgment derived from a long tenure of judicial
office, pronounced in Napoleon's case the following verdict, with
which any objective mind must surely agree:

> It is not mine to record the glories of Waterloo, and there was no
> memorable occurrence within my humble sphere, till, on Napoleon
> being brought captive in an English ship-of-war to Plymouth, the
> question arose, how this person was to be disposed of? Lord Ellen-
> borough, Sir William Grant, Sir William Scott, and other great

[1] John Campbell (1781–1861) Barrister, M.P., Solicitor and Attorney-General,
Lord Chancellor of Ireland 1841; Chief Justice of the Queen's Bench in 1850;
Lord Chancellor of England 1859. One of the best judges of his day, and author
of memoirs that are still read.

jurists being consulted, they gave conflicting and very unsatis-
factory opinions with respect to the law of nations upon the 'status'
of the Emperor—some saying he was to be regarded as a prisoner
of war—others as a subject of Louis XVIII, to whom he should be
delivered up to be tried for treason—and others as a pirate or a
hostis humani generis carrying about with him a *caput lupinum*—
while there were not wanting persons so romantically liberal as to
contend that, having thrown himself on our hospitality, he was
entitled to immediate freedom, and that he should be allowed to
range at pleasure over the earth. I think Lord Eldon took a much
more sensible view of the subject than any of them—which was
'that the case was not provided for by anything to be found in
Grotius or Vattel, but that the law of self-preservation would
justify the keeping of him under restraint in some distant region,
where he should be treated with all indulgence compatible with a
due regard for the peace of mankind'.

Accordingly, St Helena was selected as the place of his exile;
and to put a stop to all experiments in our Courts, by writs of
habeas corpus, or actions for false imprisonment, an Act of Parliament was passed to legalize his detention. Had the disgraceful
disputes been avoided, which afterwards took place respecting the
number of bottles of wine he should be allowed for dinner, and the
domiciliary visits to which he should be liable, I believe that his
captivity at Longwood would have brought no impeachment on
British justice or generosity, either in his own age or with posterity.
As things were managed, I am afraid it will be said that he was
treated, in the eighteenth century, with the same cruel spirit as the
Maid of Orleans was in the fifteenth: and there may be tragedies
on the Death of Napoleon, in which Sir Hudson Lowe will be the
Sbirro—and even Lord Eldon may be introduced as the pitiless
Old Councillor who decreed the hero's imprisonment.

A Select Bibliography

Principal Sources
Bibliothèque Nationale, Paris
British Museum (Department of Manuscripts)
Record Office
Royal Archives, Windsor
Contemporary English journals

The following is a selection of the principal works consulted:
Allardyce, A. *Memoirs of Viscount Keith* (London, Edinburgh, 1882)
Allen, Sir Carleton *John Scott, Earl of Eldon* (London, 1928)
Aubry, Octave *Sainte-Hélène* (Paris, 1935)
Beker or Becker *Relation de la Mission du Général Comte Beker auprès de l'Empereur Napoléon depuis la seconde abdication jusqu'au passage à bord du 'Bellerophon'* (Paris, 1841)
Bory de Saint Vincent, J-B. *Voyage dans les quatre principales îles des mers d'Afrique* (Paris, 1801)
Bertrand, Maréchal Comte *Cahiers de Sainte-Hélène* (Paris, 1960)
Bunbury, Sir Henry *Lives of the Chancellors of the Privy Seal*
Dechamps, Jules, *Napoléon à Plymouth et l'ordonnance d'Habeas Corpus du Lord Chief Justice d'Angleterre, in 'Bulletin de l'Académie Royale de Belgique'*, (1955)
Dicey, A. V. *The Law of the Constitution*, 8th Ed. (London, 1885)
Dunan, Marcel *Napoléon et l'Habeas Corpus, in 'Bulletin de l'Institut Napoleon'* (1955)
Ganière, Paul *Napoléon à Sainte-Hélène* (Paris, 1956)
Gourgaud, Général Baron *Journal* (Paris, 1819, réédité 1944)
Houssaye, Henry (1815, 19me ed. Paris, 1914)
Lallemand, Ch., Général Baron *Manuscrit conservé par le Baron d'Archer de Montgascon, 'The French–American Review', édité par l'Institut Français de Washington*
Las Cases, Comte de *Memorial de Sainte-Hélène* (Paris, 1822)
Lyttelton, Neville S. *Conversation with Napoleon* (Revue Bleue, 8 September, 1894)
Lofft, Capell *Morning Chronicle* (July 30th, August 10th, 1815)
Maitland, Sir Frederick *Narrative of the Surrender of Buonaparte and his residence on board H.M.S. Bellerophon* (London, 1826)
Marchand, J. G. Comte *Mémoires* (Paris, 1952)
Montholon, Comte de *Récits de la captivité de l'Empereur Napoléon à Sainte-Hélène* (Paris, 1847)
Planat de la Faye *Vie, Souvenirs, Lettres et Dictées de Napoléon* (Paris, 1897)

Rosebery, Earl of *The Last Phase* (London, 1906)
Romilly, Sir Samuel *Life and Works* (1908)
Savant, Jean *Tel fut Fouché* (Paris, 1950)
Scott, Sir Walter *Life of Napoleon* (London, 1849)
Silvestre, J. *De Waterloo à Sainte-Hélène* (1904)
Thiers, Adolphe *Histoire du Consulat et de l'Empire* (Paris, 1883)
Twiss *Life of Lord Eldon*
Yonge, C. D. *Life of Lord Liverpool*

Index